Praise for *Meet Mr. Smith*

"Awe-inspiring . . . extraordinary . . . this book is a gem!"
—*Rachel, 21, Concord, NH*

"The most wholesome, noble, and God-exalting book on sexuality in the past twenty years . . . utterly remarkable . . . this book will change people's lives."
—*Ben, 20, Aurora, CO*

"WOW!!! . . . Loved it beyond words! . . . one of the most important books that anyone could read, married or single! . . . Since I received this manuscript I have read it three times."
—*Aimee, 30, South Weber, UT*

"Ludy-esque" . . . incredible! . . . by far, the best book they have written!"
—*Mary, 26, Fayetteville, AR*

"I honestly have not read a book quite like it . . . transparent . . . deeply touching."
—*Amy, 28, Tolono, IL*

"Absolutely phenomenal."
—*Ryan, 27, Chattanooga, TN*

"A can't-put-it-down book . . . so imaginative and visionary . . . a radical call."
—*Michael, 39, Orlando, FL*

"Eye-opening . . . engaging . . . original . . . keeps you guessing."
—*Hannah, 23, Beaverton, OR*

"An incredible twist."
—*Sarah, 22, Edmonton, Alberta, Canada*

"Profound . . . vulnerable . . . honest . . . an incredible journey . . .
It is imperative that you meet Mr. Smith!"
—*Tiffany, 19, Spokane, WA*

"A treasure trove . . . unprecedented . . . poignant . . . humorous . . .
profound . . . I could not possibly recommend it highly enough."
—*Bethany, 22, Selma, OR*

"Fresh . . . funny . . . useful."
—*Tim, 22, Thonotosassa, FL*

"This book is brilliant! . . . unique . . . imaginative . . . catchy and
fun . . . strongly gets the point across . . . Only God could inspire
such a book."
—*Amy, 21, Escondido, CA*

"Especially for me . . . everything I want . . . gave me the same
feeling I have whenever I watch *Braveheart.*"
—*Levi, 23, Rio Lindo, CA*

"Amazing . . . a taste of heaven on earth . . . ingenious . . . a witty
page-turner."
—*Kendra, 22, Ephrata, PA*

"More beautiful than a fairy tale . . . evokes the most honest tears
. . . magnificent . . . like any great story of adventure, beauty,
mystery, and love, you will not be able to put it down."
—*Courtney, 20, Oxford, MI*

"Intriguing . . . a large dose of flair . . . very refreshing!"
—*Nadine, 26, Adelaide, Australia*

"Chock-full of truth and practical relationship advice . . . I could
not put this book down . . . enchanting."
—*Lindsay, 27, Billings, MT*

MEET
MR. SMITH

REVOLUTIONIZE THE WAY YOU THINK ABOUT SEX, PURITY, AND ROMANCE

Eric & Leslie Ludy

THOMAS NELSON
Since 1798

NASHVILLE DALLAS MEXICO CITY RIO DE JANEIRO BEIJING

Published in Nashville, Tennessee, by Thomas Nelson. Thomas Nelson is a trademark of Thomas Nelson, Inc.

Published in association with Loyal Arts Literary Agency, www.LoyalArts.com.

Thomas Nelson, Inc. titles may be purchased in bulk for educational, business, fund-raising, or sales promotional use. For information, please e-mail SpecialMarkets@ThomasNelson.com.

Unless otherwise marked, Scripture quotations are taken from the King James Version of the Bible.

Scripture quotations marked NASB are taken from The New American Standard Bible®, © 1960, 1977, 1995 by the Lockman Foundation. Used by permission.

Library of Congress Cataloging-in-Publication Data

Ludy, Eric.
    Meet Mr. Smith : revolutionize the way you think about sex, purity, and romance / Eric and Leslie Ludy.
       p. cm.
    Includes bibliographical references (p. 229).
    ISBN 978-0-8499-0543-8 (pbk.)
    1. Sex—Religious aspects—Christianity. 2. Christians—Sexual behavior.
3. Single people—Sexual behavior. I. Ludy, Leslie. II. Title. III. Title: Meet Mister Smith.
BT708.L83 2007
241'.66—dc22

2007032729

Printed in the United States of America
07 08 09 10 11 RRD 6 5 4 3 2 1

Contents

PART 2
Leslie

A Word Before— from Leslie

This is an unusual book. My husband is to be thanked for that. Sometimes Eric's book ideas get shot down in publisher board meetings, but this one surprisingly slipped through. And I am so glad it did.

At first, I was reticent to participate in a book about finding Great Sex. This is a rather awkward topic to even *read* a book on, let alone *write* a book on. Leave it to the gregarious, never-to-roll-over-and-play-dead Eric Ludy to convince me we should tackle it.

The story you are about to read in part one of this book is *almost* completely true. I will admit that Beef (my pet name for Eric) fudged the actual events a little in some instances, but as hard as it will be for you to believe, this bizarre story is based on actual events that unfolded in our lives and marriage during the past twelve weeks. Let me repeat: what you are about to read is true . . . *sort of.*

During the next seventeen chapters I will peek in and out of the pages a few times, but all in all, part one is Eric's territory. Then, in part two, I offer a female perspective on some tough questions our generation is currently asking.

We hope you enjoy this journey. And, as a result of this story, may you never think a lowly thought about Great Sex ever again!

PART 1

Eric

CHAPTER 1

Imposter Sex

Just yesterday I sat down at a Starbucks in downtown Manhattan and had a very uncomfortable three-and-a-half minute conversation with Sex.

I realize that sounds a bit odd. And I assure you, *odd* is not a strong enough word to describe the experience.

As you know, Sex is a rather popular celebrity in our modern world, and it is easier, these days, to book the Dalai Lama for a keynote address on "The Beauty and Wonder of War" than to book Sex for an interview. His docket is crammed full with everything from nude photo shoots at the Playboy mansion, to steamy love scenes on the silver screen, to guest appearances on *Howard Stern*.

Let me give you a little background to help you understand what led to my conversation with Sex.

I have certain connections gained through my writing career, and I decided to cash in on one of the favors owed me.

Yesterday, I caught wind that Sex would be on a movie set in a Manhattan high-rise. And after pulling a few strings, I was able to get a friend of a friend of a friend to slip a note to his agent.

The note read:

My name is Eric Ludy. I'm writing a book that will expose everything. I know you are an imposter. If you wish to defend your name, then give me a call. My cell number is . . .

The message was short, but it accomplished its errand. Later that day, I received a phone call.

"Mr. Ludy?" The man's voice was raspy and condescending.

"Yes?" I answered. I could hear what sounded like a large piece of gum being mercilessly masticated in his mouth.

"Sex doesn't have time for your games!" the man insisted.

"This isn't a game," I said firmly. "I have hard evidence proving him a fraud. And I'm going public with it."

There was a long pause.

"He'll give you two minutes. The Ritz-Carlton, presidential suite, one o'clock tomorrow."

"No!" I insisted. "I want five minutes. Have him meet me at the Starbucks at 45th and Broadway, Manhattan, three o'clock today."

With that I hung up, feeling adrenaline explode through my veins. I'd seen people talk tough like that in the movies, but I'd never tried it in real life. It was sort of fun.

I was confident he would show. When you have that much to lose, you will do a lot to keep your secrets.

□ □ □

Sex.

Just study that short little word for a moment. Why does such a dwarfish word garner so much of our attention? I mean, if you think about it, *sex* is a very unimpressive word. If anything, it sounds oddly similar to a name you might give your dog, not the title you'd give to your life's great ambition. *Sex* boasts merely three letters, yet it struts about the stage of life as if it were ten boldfaced capital letters leaving four exclamation points in its wake.

Sex.

Take another moment and ponder that stumpy little word. It sits on our minds like a plump kitty preening itself, making it seem impossible for us to move without incurring a serious amount of scratches. But that's just it. Why does Sex have such a hold on us? Why are we such pushovers for its chicanery? When we sit down at the kitchen table in the morning, unfold the newspaper, and begin reading a fabulous editorial, why do we allow this overfed feline to jump up on the table and plant itself right smack in the middle of our attention?

Sex.

I realize the word, just like that plump cat, has a beautiful fluffy coat, purrs like a idling Maserati engine, and possesses an intoxicating ferocity—but let's not forget the set of teeth and claws these three letters are packing.

□ □ □

Just yesterday I sat down in a Starbucks café on Broadway with this overfed feline, and the two of us had a heart-to-heart.

The place was packed, as usual, with an eclectic array of people sipping caffeinated beverages while typing on laptops, chatting with friends, or sealing business deals. Those of you who have spent time in Starbucks know it is possible to eaves-drop on at least five conversations at any given time if the con-versation you find yourself in isn't suiting your fancy. In other words, it's crowded and close—sort of like an elevator ride to the seventy-seventh floor of the Chrysler Building.

Although the environment wasn't much to Sex's liking, see-ing as how I had threatened to expose his impostership, he arrived, nevertheless, with two bodyguards and a haughty smirk splattered all over his face, as if he had left the lid off the blender that morning when mixing up his daily dose of self-importance.

My first glance of him came through the Starbucks' picture window as I noticed him with his bodyguards out near the curb. I was quite surprised at his appearance. Seeing as how this guy is all about glitz and glam, I'd expected a handsome, well-formed leading man sort of fellow—you know, Tom Cruise meets Russell Crowe. However, this guy was more like a smarmy Elvis impersonator. He was almost cartoonish in his form—tall and lean, but with a blubbery beer bulge up front. Although he had a rather attractive face, his hair was greasy black and he even had a set of long sideburns à la "the King."

□ □ □

Sex.

It's an inglorious, diminutive word with a supremely cock-sure personality. You know that one kid who sat next to you in earth science class in the eighth grade? I think his name was Dillon. You know, the one who smacked his gum like a masticating bovine and glopped a pound of hair gel onto his head every morning. The kid had a way about him. The girls fainted with breathless wonder as he strode down the hallway, and the guys grunted their approval as he strutted by their lockers. Well, Dillon never studied for tests, because he knew you would. So for forty-five test-taking minutes of misery, you found yourself choking back revulsion as Dillon's overapplication of Polo cologne and his unmistakable Twinkie-breath hung like a cloud about your right shoulder—well, *that's Sex*. It struts, it preens, it croons, it hovers, it cheats, it's drenched in buckets of Polo cologne—and when it gets caught, it doesn't mind bringing you down right along with it.

◻ ◻ ◻

I can now say, from personal experience, that Sex doesn't make a very good interview. As I sat at a small table near the street-side windows of the café, nursing a tasty chunk of coffee cake and a tall chai tea, one of his bodyguards approached me. He mumbled, "Are you Mr. Ludy?"

"Yes, I am."

"Come with me," he commanded. Something about his con-descending voice sounded oddly familiar.

"I don't think so," I responded. "We're meeting here. He might as well get used to me talking about these things in public."

After a protracted dirty look and a blue streak of profanity, the bodyguard turned and headed back through the front door of the café and out into the street, where Sex was waiting.

I watched the interchange through the window with inter-est. Sex was obviously used to getting his way with people and was not one to kowtow to the whim of a peon like myself. He cursed and stomped a few times in anger; then he took a deep breath, lifted his chin into the air as if the idea of entering a Starbucks was beneath him, and commanded his bodyguards to open the door for his entry.

As Sex entered, it seemed the entire room stopped and looked. You would have thought a Greek god was humbling himself and dining among mere mortals.

"He's gorgeous!" I heard a woman whisper from somewhere behind my right shoulder.

"That dude is a *dude!*" said a male voice near the coffee pickup counter.

I thought it odd that someone so unimpressive to me was receiving such accolades from these coffee drinkers.

Flanked by his imposing bodyguards, Sex sauntered up to my table and looked down at me with disdain.

◻ ◻ ◻

Sex.

It's a word that captures your attention, gets you excited, traps you in its web, makes you feel guilty, and messes up your life all in the span of ten minutes.

Sex.

I realize you may not see Sex the way I do. To you, he may not appear as a greasy Elvis impersonator with a jiggling midsection. My eyesight has been altered ever since I saw the truth. Things that used to draw me like a moth to a flame now seem supremely corny and unattractive. So I understand if you disagree with me on this matter as we start out this book. You may very well see Imposter Sex as the "gorgeous dude among dudes" if he were to swagger into the Starbucks in your hometown.

However, I must forewarn you: don't buy his charm. For all his smooth, "Babe, I love you's," he's a con, a thief, a crook—and not a very socially adroit one at that.

□ □ □

"So you're the loser who caused me to miss my afternoon rub-down, huh?" he said with disdain.

I stood up and held out my hand for a handshake, but Sex grimaced as if repulsed by my sort of life form.

I dropped my hand to my side. "Thanks for coming," I said politely.

"The clock's ticking," he barked, "so get out whatever it is you supposedly have on me." He pulled out a chair and situated his bulging midsection into the small seat. His body-guards stood on either side of him, keeping close watch on the people in the café—including me.

I sat back down and gathered my thoughts. My soul was trembling, although I would say I held myself together fairly convincingly on the outside. And despite Sex's arrogant, gruff demeanor, I could sense that he was nervous.

"The jig's up!" I announced. "I've found the real thing, and I have a publisher willing to print the whole exposé. We're blowing this wide open!"

Sex looked at me as if he thought I was insane. "Mr. Ludy," he said evenly, "have you gone mad?"

"I'm perfectly lucid, sir, I can assure you."

"Well, I'm convinced that you've completely lost your

mind." He leaned back in his chair with a condescending smile. "First of all," he continued, "I'm the real thing, and I've got a billion-dollar industry willing to back up my claims." He chuckled derisively. "And second of all, even if you did find my nemesis, which I highly doubt, rumor has it that he's a doddering old fool. From what I hear, he couldn't get a rabbit to reproduce if you loaded him intravenously with ten gallons of Viagra!"

I couldn't wait to wipe that smug expression off his face. "But I don't just *know* that he exists, sir," I said calmly. "I've experienced the results of his work firsthand."

I let that sink in for a moment.

Sex leaned over and whispered something in his bodyguard's ear. The bodyguard nodded at his partner, and then the two large, muscular men left the café.

All-important Sex then turned and looked at me with knives in his gaze. "You're wasting my time, kid."

"I'm bringing this all out into the open! Everything! The world is going to know that you are nothing more than an imposter."

He paused and then leaned closer to me. "What do you want from me?" he hissed, lowering his voice. "Money?"

"Absolutely not. That's not why I am here."

"Well, then, what did you expect to accomplish with this amateur display of politicking?"

"I just want you to know that your jig is up."

At that moment a bright red Ferrari Scaglietti squealed to a halt in front of the Starbucks' curb.

"Mr. Ludy," Sex announced as he rose from his chair, "my jig will never be up!"

Sex.

Yes, it's only three letters long, but it may very well be the most powerful word around today. Those three letters have caused more havoc than *chocolate, caffeine, nicotine, gambling, Nintendo Wii,* and *butternut toffee ice cream* all combined and multiplied by twenty-six. Sex is one bad dude. He's got a rap sheet longer than Jessie James and a wily smirk to match it.

Sex.

Sure, he is legally allowed to share a bed with you and your spouse. But let's be ruthlessly honest here. Sex must be quite a miserable character, because, as excited as most married couples are to have him hang out with them on their honeymoon, it sure does seem like the guy wears out his welcome awfully fast.

Sex.

Strangely, these three letters weren't always smarmy, conniving, and falsely debonair. I know this may be difficult to believe, but Sex wasn't originally coupled with strip clubs, nudie magazines, adulterous antics, and sipping rum punch in a penthouse apartment near Hollywood and Vine. In fact, there was a time when Sex was a clean-shaven gentleman, mature, dignified, bearing roses, and speaking in poetic rhymes with a hint of a British accent. There was a time when Sex worked humbly and selflessly to bring about something good, pleasurable, fun, noble, and pleasing to God.

What happened to this Sex, you ask? I must forewarn you, there are myriad theories, of which I will only mention a couple. Many theorists hold to the Darth Vader legend, which imagines that Sex—a dashing young dude with an Elvis-like flop of hair and long sideburns—one day realized his true power and magnetic potential and gave into the dark side. There is a smaller band of conspiracy theorists who claim that the original, dignified Sex mysteriously died back in 1960 and that his son, Sex Jr. (the spittin' image of his father), has carried on his father's family business ever since. This is commonly known as the *junior theory*. There have been several other theories passed around over the centuries—some preposterous, some deranged, some quite hokey, and some actually conceivable. But there is one theory that few in our modern times have ever heard. I call this theory *the amazing truth*.

I agree, the theory I'm about to propose is a bit fantastical, but what in regard to Sex isn't? And it is important to note that the difference between this and the other preposterous, deranged, and hokey theories out there is that this idea can actually be tested and proven to be true. Therefore, this really isn't a theory at all but a fantastical fact.

So let me lay out for you the fantastical facts about Sex.

I can demonstrate to you that the smarmy, lust-crazed Sex we all know today is an imposter and a backstabbing traitor who has lied to all of us about the true nature of Sex and duped us all into thinking he is the only Sex out there. But there *is* another version of Sex! I realize this may sound a bit unbelievable, but the original, refined rendition of Sex is still alive. I've personally encountered his grandeur; in fact, I'm quite familiar with his work. He doesn't have an Elvis-like flop of hair and long sideburns, he doesn't have a jiggling bulge around his middle, and he doesn't swivel his hips—I'd say he's more William Wallace meets Lord Alfred Tennyson, with a dash of Jimmy Stewart and a dripping dollop of Sidney Poitier.

The original version of Sex is something to behold. In fact, he makes Imposter Sex look like potato skins in yesterday's trash. But our hero has been obscured for many years by cultural ignorance, and the path leading to his chalet needs a little dusting off before I can walk you up to his front door.

□ □ □

As Sex roared away in his bright red sports car, I smiled to myself. I had never done anything so Clint Eastwood—you know, staring down a villain and calling his bluff. But I was hoping to see him sweat. I wanted to see his expression when I told him that I had experienced firsthand the work of the original version of Sex. I wanted to see the guy up close and analyze what it is about him that people find so attractive.

Once you've met the original version, I promise you, Imposter Sex looks like a chump. Sure, he's handsome in a Las Vegas sort of way, but he's nothing more than a wannabe version of the real thing. There is a better version of Sex, a *far* better version. In fact, my plan in this book is to negotiate an interview with the real version of this three-letter word, get him in his finest attire, and just let him speak for himself. I'm confident that when you behold him, you will find that the word *better* falls far short of what this version of Sex actually is. Prepare to utter words like *Wow!* and *Whoa!* as we reveal the real version of Sex through the pages of this book.

□ □ □

Sex.

Let's admit it. This crazy little word fascinates us. We can't ignore it, we can't turn it off—we hear the word, see the word, and stumble over the word in nearly every situation life brings our way. It pesters us, tempts us, intrigues us, and destroys us. We love it, we hate it; we love to love it, hate to love it, and love to hate it. So I'm fairly confident that you will enjoy this book. Because this book will do for your mentality on Sex what *Extreme Makeover* does for the toothless and misshapen—it will transform it into a beautiful rose. You'll see Sex like you've never seen him before—the original Sex, the one who inspired such phrases as "once upon a time" and "happily ever after."

I'm guessing you are excited to be introduced to my friend, the original Sex, but for reasons of necessity, I'm afraid that will have to wait a little while. It is important that we first deal with the imposter. You see, Imposter Sex (the sly character I met with at Starbucks) is a wily rascal who doesn't appreciate what I am doing to his reputation in this book. Imposter Sex thrives off ignorance. But he shrivels up and fades away when we expose him for what he really is—a shameless wannabe.

CHAPTER 2

Jimmy the Shrimp

Have you ever thought, *Life would be a whole lot easier if Sex just didn't exist*? None of us actually wishes Sex didn't exist, of course, but still, if we hog-tie our hormones and look at life through a purely rational pair of glasses, eliminating Sex from life's equation makes a whole lot of sense.

Let's put ourselves in the Creator's chair for a second. We are making a great big world, full of all sorts of exciting things—but we want our people to be good, upstanding, honorable, self-less, and bear a certain measure of dignity. So when the Garden of Eden comes into view and it's time to craft our very first human being, it just makes sense—knowing what we know now—that we should leave out the excretory and the reproductive systems. After all, those two systems lead to 100 percent of all the dirty jokes worldwide (OK, there are a few associated with burping) and are the leading cause of everything smelly and perverted in this world. It seems that, if we were to sit in the

Captain's chair, we could do the world a whole lot of good by making humans excrete and reproduce like sweet daffodils rather than sweaty animals.

Sex just makes everything a bit problematic.

The other morning, I was headed to the health club to get some exercise. It was a frosty morning, and I was intentional before leaving the house to slip on some long underwear beneath my sweatpants, knowing that the trek from frigid parking lot to indoor warmth can be a long one. After I parked, I worked up an inner resolve to face the chill and hopped out of the car.

As I walked to the building, I gritted my teeth and attempted to maintain a calm exterior as my body shivered. Meanwhile, a guy with a shag of reddish hair hopped out of a Toyota truck and joined me in the long trek. But whereas I was bundled to the nines with coat, gloves, and even long underwear, this guy was wearing *shorts*. I gasped with horror, and before I could analyze and thusly quash the words I was about to launch from my squawk box, I blurted, "How do you pull off those shorts?"

Sex creates problems we certainly wouldn't have if it didn't exist.

The guy in the shorts looked at me in revulsion, as I fumbled for a different way to express my very unnecessary question. I mean, did I really need to know how this guy could pull off wearing shorts on a cold day? I don't think so! As far as he was concerned, I was not only a sexual deviant but a rather rude one at that. My point is, Sex caused that very uncomfortable scene!

Sex makes for awkward moments that a Sexless world just wouldn't have.

A Sexless world would be a safer world, an easier world, and a more open world, albeit a much blander (and less populated) world. If you remove Sex from the equation of life, then you don't have sexual sin, you don't have rape, you don't have unwanted pregnancy, you don't have venereal disease, and you don't have guys in shorts thinking you throw around really bad pickup lines. But you also don't have a dimension in life that adds dazzling color, vibrant intimacy, and a sense of rich and meaningful closeness.

If we're still sitting in the Creator's chair, I say, for now, let's keep Sex around and try to think of another divine way of handling the problem.

What about making Sex extremely uncomfortable, even painful? I know that isn't the most pleasant thought, but just think about the effect. You see, a certain dimension of Sex is pleasure, so it seems reasonable to blame all the problems with Sex on that pleasure dimension. Wouldn't you agree that God would have been wholly justified in making Sex a miserable experience? If Sex were miserable, then the only people participating in it would be people serious about having babies. Rape, unwanted pregnancy, and venereal disease would radically decrease the moment Sex lost its pleasure value. I'm guessing painful Sex would not be popular, and as a result maybe it would also not be a problem—unless you call pain a problem.

However, I must admit that painful Sex really wouldn't solve the root problem with Sex. Because the real problem with Sex isn't the concept or the action of Sex itself; the problem with Sex is what stands behind Sex controlling its behavior. Just like the bigger-than-life robot marching through the streets of Manhattan, it's the guy holding the remote control who's really to blame for all the laser-blasted cars and buildings turned to dust. Sex isn't a lone gunman—someone else is driving the show, calling the shots, and Sex is merely the flunky, the patsy, the lackey.

You know how in mobster movies, you find out that the Mob has been laundering money through a series of front companies, and no one knew that Jimmy the Shrimp from the west side of Chicago was actually the deviant behind the whole murderous affair? The problem with Sex is a lot like that. There's a Jimmy the Shrimp behind this whole Sex thing, and it's making the whole bottle of milk go sour. And whether Sex was removed from the picture entirely or the act of Sex actually became painful, the problem (aka Jimmy the Shrimp) would still be at large, finding himself a new flunky and creating a new front behind which to hide his deviant behavior. Sex just happens to be his chosen front.

You see, Sex is kind of like that kid in the first grade who sneezed, coughed, and dribbled his influenza all over the entire classroom. The kid was an infection waiting to happen. Yellow stuff oozed from his nose like half-congealed lemon Jell-O, and what didn't find its way down the front of his chin was wiped indecorously upon his sleeve. It would be easy to blame the kid for infecting you—after all, he's the one who refused to cover his mouth when he coughed in your face, and yes, he's also the one who grabbed your hand with his goopy fingers in an effort to steal your beloved hacky sack. But let's remember something here—the snot-nosed kid is *not* the actual problem. Yes, he needs a few lessons in manners and needs to be scrubbed up a bit, but the real problem is the sickness he is carrying. The kid is a carrier of a sickness just as Sex is a carrier of a problem. *Sex is not the problem itself.* In fact, remove the sickness from this little kid and teach him how to cover his mouth and blow his nose and *voilà!* You've got yourself a nice little boy with rosy cheeks as sweet as pink Kool-Aid on a hot summer's day.

Sex is hacking and coughing and covered in half-congealed lemonlike snot, but the solution is not to throw out Sex in our modern world or to genetically alter it so that it becomes a miserable experience. Rather, the solution is to find a way to get Sex healthy again. So let's talk about this "sickness" that Sex is carrying, because truly that is the problem for which we need to find a solution. If we could expose Jimmy the Shrimp, then maybe we could pin him down with some tax evasion scheme and get him in cuffs.

Selfishness.

Yep. That's the sickness; that's the problem. It's that's simple to describe. Selfishness (aka Jimmy the Shrimp) is the essence of everything wrong, not just with Sex, but with everything else on planet earth. I know the word *selfishness* doesn't sound too menacing. We all know selfishness can make for little messes in life, but sometimes we don't realize how deadly it actually is. To blame the breakdown of Sex and the breakdown of society on detestable words like *murder, hate, holocaust, slander, genocide, betrayal,* or *crooked lawyers* at least makes the story a bit more believable. But blaming it on selfishness? Come on! Isn't selfishness one of those things four-year-olds are warned not to have, so they can grow up to be decent kids who share their toys? Selfishness can't possibly be the problem behind every other problem on planet earth, can it?

Selfishness, like Jimmy the Shrimp, works underground. Most people don't even realize it is there, which is precisely why it is so dangerous. Selfishness works in secret, behind closed doors, on the black market, plotting and planning our destruction. Selfishness is the Mob boss of the soul. In fact, without selfishness, you wouldn't have murder, hate, holocaust, slander, genocide, betrayal, or crooked lawyers—because those are all the convoluted results of Jimmy the Shrimp's regime. Simply put, selfishness is the sickness behind all other sicknesses.

Let's define *selfishness* so we are all on the same page.

When you were born, God entrusted you with a body. Who owns and operates that body? *You* do.

Let's do a little exercise and look in a mirror. You see that hand waving back at you—that's *your* hand. And that nose—it's *yours* too. Yep, and that's your big toe, your left earlobe, and your right eyebrow. If you wish, you can make your hand snatch up of a pile of wet snow, form it into a snowball, and throw it across the lawn, striking your younger brother right smack in the face. Of course, you may or may not choose to do such a devilish thing, but the point is, it is *you*, and not someone else, who is in charge of your hand and, amazingly, your hand does precisely what you command it to do, whether you ask it to perform a good deed or a bad one. As a result of this extraordinary power position that you hold, you can make your body do anything, go anywhere, or say anything you want it to (within certain natural bounds, of course). You are king of this little castle called *you*.

At first glance, this whole you-being-king thing sounds kind of nice. But there's a little wrinkle to your royalty. Yes, you are in control, you are king, but there is something that is still king over you, and even though it seems like you are in control of this thing called life, you are actually not. There is a Mob boss you report to. There's a rotund, greasy-cheeked guy smoking a

Cuban cigar and pacing around inside your being who actually calls the shots. This dude has many names. We've been calling him Jimmy the Shrimp, but historically his name is the Flesh. And note to self: the Flesh is a nasty, nasty dude.

At first, the realization that you are king of your castle was probably exhilarating. You may have grown up under the dictatorial rule of strict parents, and the discovery of your own personal power came like a shot of ecstasy to your system. You may have even tried your hand at a little experimental sin, just to prove to yourself, "Yes! I am really in control here!" You may have toyed with a bit of debauchery and swung the bat of lust around a few times and knocked the sheen off of your purity.

But if you haven't yet figured out the catch, you soon will. You see, the catch is, you are free as a bird to do bad, mischievous, crude, and debased things, but you are *not* free to do godly things. Being loving, pure, kind, and good-hearted doesn't seem like much of an ambition until you realize that no matter how hard you try, you can't pull it off. You are stuck on a one-way street called Sin, and there's no going the other way. You may want to be noble, to be forgiving, to be peaceful, to be victorious over sin, to be selfless and consider someone else's needs above your own, but you can only show a surface goodness, because on the inside it's all about *you*—what *you* want, how it makes *you* feel, how it makes *you* look better, and how it fosters value in *your* own personal investment portfolio.

It's a scary thing to stare your potential for being bad in the face. And it is also a distressing thing to stare your inability to be truly good in the face. Many of you, after seeing how easy it is to be bad, have maybe gotten a little shaken up. You want to correct the downward moral spiral of your life, but the Shrimp's got you. While you thought you were in control of your life, you were actually doing his bidding.

Selfishness is you having the gall to actually sit in the president's brown leather chair and try to rule over your life as if you were, in fact, the real authority. You are not the rightful authority over your life; *God is*. But you sat down in the chair and claimed it for yourself. And this action of subversion and rebellion against God authorized a new power to take over your existence—and the Shrimp moved into that illustrious power position. It's legally his now, and as a result, you find yourself sitting in a position of power but in actuality wielding really no power of your own whatsoever, because when you try to change your position and get up out of that brown leather chair—*you can't*.

You see, God designed us humans to be governed; therefore, something will always be in control of us—and that something is either going to be Jimmy the Shrimp or the God of the universe.

Like in every good mobster movie, one of the mobsters wants out. He's tired of the corruption and he wants to live his life rightly; he wants to live by a better value system. But of course, the drama centers on the fact that the Mob will never let him leave because he knows too much. Likewise, the Shrimp won't listen to your whining. He doesn't care at all about your high ideals and about the fact that you want to love and serve and contribute to society. Many years ago, in the Garden of Eden, the wily Satan negotiated for the Shrimp to gain authority over your soul, and no hot, salty tears and pouting lips on your part are going to win your freedom. Believe me, it's been tried.

So getting back to Sex, this is precisely why Sex is so convoluted in our modern world. Sex is a carrier for Jimmy the Shrimp's agenda. You may want Sex to exhibit the beauty and romance of heaven in your life, but as long as the Shrimp stands behind it, Sex will always only be selfish, lust-driven, and perverse.

We need to somehow escape the Mob.

What can we do about the Shrimp? Can we turn over state's evidence on the scoundrel and enter some kind of spiritual witness protection program? Can we arouse some sort of organized attack within and kick the weasel out of there?

It's been tried. The most well-meaning men and women throughout history have tried their hardest to launch a coup on the Shrimp in order to allow nobility, love, dignity, peace, and purity to reign in their bodies. For some reason, human beings just can't muster up the strength to overcome the power of selfishness in the soul. You may not want to sit in that brown leather chair of power anymore, but the reality is, you are superglued down, and you are officially messing up your life more and more each and every day as long as you preside over your existence.

Selfishness is a messy, miserable problem. But there is a way out.

Depending upon how serious you are about being free from the Shrimp, there is a way to escape the Mob and become a good guy. But it's not easy. It involves giving up your life as you now know it. It involves giving the brown leather chair back to God and allowing Him to rule your life from this day forward. If you try to tackle Jimmy the Shrimp on your own, he'll cut you. But the Shrimp trembles before Jesus Christ. All Jesus

Christ has to do is step into your inner castle, and Jimmy the Shrimp loses his power over you.

Remember, there is no such thing as you being in control of your life without being under the thumb of the Shrimp or under the thumb of God. You will be ruled. The choice is yours: whom will you serve?

◻ ◻ ◻

Sex.

It's Jimmy the Shrimp's number one weapon to destroy each of our lives.

Sex.

It's God's number one proving ground for building His children into heroes of His grace and glory. Whereas Jimmy the Shrimp might twist Imposter Sex into something people can trip over, God designed Great Sex as something to fight for and wrestle to achieve.

Sex.

It's not bad in and of itself, but if it is driven by selfishness, it will destroy not only our lives but also the lives of many others.

Sex.

It's waiting to be rediscovered in all its majesty and beauty. And that will only happen when it is animated by the life of Christ ruling within the human body.

Sex.

There are two versions. The Imposter, ruled by Jimmy the Shrimp, and the real thing, ruled by Jesus the Christ. I hope it's clear which one you should pursue.

Sex.

It has the potential either to ruin your life or to be one of the great rewards of your existence. You can't find Great Sex on your own, but you can choose to allow God to bring it into your life.

◻ ◻ ◻

This is a very simple book built upon a very simple premise: God designed us as sexual beings and invented the idea of sex for a glorious purpose. This issue in our lives can prove messy, uncomfortable, and often even destructive—but it is our hope that through our journey together we can transform this topic into one that inspires extraordinary hope, great excitement, premarriage bliss, and lifelong marital beauty.

If you are looking for support from the Shrimp, be forewarned, he's not a big fan of the contents of this book. You will probably have a few scraps and scrapes with your Flesh over this message, but we can assure you, the end result of such a struggle is more than worth it.

Great Sex.

We all like the sound of those two words together. The word *great* denotes the very best version of something—and of course, when you attach that to *sex*, you have an irresistible combination.

This book is about how to find Great Sex. This isn't a book about cooking asparagus or building toy rocket ships. For those interested in how-to instruction manuals, this may prove rather disappointing. This is more of a "map to buried treasure" sort of experience.

Let me give you one piece of advice as we board the ship and head off into the open seas on this adventure. Don't expect the treasure of God's kingdom to be sitting out in the open for every

Tom, Dick, and Harry to pick up and lug away. It's buried treasure, for which you need a map.

And just like every good treasure-hunting adventure movie, be expecting the scalawag Jimmy the Shrimp to make a solemn vow to stop you on this journey. After all, what's a great adventure without an antagonist to make the whole drama fun?

CHAPTER 3

The League

Every story has a backstory. Unfortunately, the backstory to the writing of this book is rather humiliatingly humorous. About five months ago, I sat across the table from a key decision maker at our publishing company, discussing the subject of this book. I assured him that Great Sex would, without hesitation, give me an interview. After all, Leslie and I had been ambassadorial cheerleaders for him during the past twelve years, and in our opinion, we had built quite a repertoire and had a great working relationship.

"Are you sure you can book this interview?" my publisher friend asked warily.

I chuckled confidently, placing a reassuring hand upon his shoulder. "Trust me."

I was supremely confident about writing this book. And I never once considered the preposterous notion that Great Sex might actually decline being involved.

But we all live and learn.

□ □ □

"Great Sex never does interviews!" was the curt response I received from his agent.

"Tell him it's Eric Ludy. He knows me rather well. I'm a huge advocate of his work!"

"Even if you were the pope, Mr. Ludy, Great Sex doesn't do interviews!" the agent insisted.

A bit frustrated, I came back the following day and placed a large manila envelope on his agent's desk, saying, "Well, could you at least give him this?"

"I will be sure to give it to him, Mr. Ludy. But please don't expect Great Sex to bend on his 'no interviews' policy."

Inside that large manila envelope I had placed the first two chapters of this book along with a sticky note that read:

Sir, I know you are a busy man, but I beg you to read this. If you change your mind about your "no interviews" policy and wish to help me deal with this current crisis over your true identity, my cell number is . . .

That was twelve long weeks ago. Eighty-four days passed before I received the call. Well, it wasn't exactly a phone call; the cryptic message was actually delivered via the deep voice of a hulking muscular behemoth. After following a mysterious blue Pontiac for over an hour into the middle of nowhere, I found myself in single-digit temperatures standing outside a quaint edifice. As he led me in through the doorway of the small, unknown structure, the large man said, "Mr. Ludy, you've got your wish. You've earned yourself an interview with Mr. Smith."

I know, I know, you are wondering who Mr. Smith is. Questions are probably shooting out your brain like water from a squirt gun. But I beg you, please, please be patient, dear reader; I can assure you, all your questions will be answered to your full satisfaction in the upcoming pages of this book. There always has to be an element of mystery when Great Sex is in the ascendant.

I had waited twelve long weeks for this interview, and to be honest, I had given up on the idea of the interview actually transpiring. Twelve weeks is a long time in the book-writing world, and book deadlines are unyielding taskmasters with no sympathy for such dilemmas. But what started out as a huge disappointment proved to be, I believe, the salvation of this manuscript. Because the absence of my number-one source on the subject forced me to look elsewhere and find additional sources in order to build my case and to write the truth about Great Sex.

In hindsight, that twelve-week delay is what ultimately made this book what it is. It created desperation, a need. The words *"Trust me, I can book this interview!"* echoed in my head with unmerciful constancy. As a result of that twelve-week delay, I ended up interviewing some unlikely characters in my journey to fill the void. I was forced to become much more colorful and creative in my approach. And I think you will find that the end result is a book that gives a lot of dimension to the concept of Great Sex.

For instance, Great Sex, contrary to popular myth, is not a singular force as is Imposter Sex. In a manner of speaking,

Great Sex is part of a team. This strange fact is something that I knew prior to penning this manuscript, but I don't believe I had ever given it a tremendous amount of thought. You see, Great Sex is the leader of an entire band of superheroes. He's sort of like Superman, in that he is in and of himself unique and powerful, but instead of "Lone Rangering" it, he works along-side other gifted characters in order to amplify his powers for the cause of good.

Those interminable twelve weeks forced me to investigate this oft-overlooked band of superheroic cohorts. And I enthusi-astically confess, it was an unexpected rabbit trail that proved wholly providential and sublime.

When I was growing up, my favorite cartoon on Saturday morning was *Super Friends*, which detailed the fabulous adven-tures of the Justice League. This legendary cartoon featured the greatest superheroes in the DC Comics universe (Superman, Wonder Woman, Aquaman, the Wonder Twins) all working together to rescue the world from evil. Well, as odd as it might seem, Great Sex heads up a very similar sort of band of protag-onists—each of them bold and brave agents of change in God's hero-making universe.

This band of heroes calls itself the *League*.

The League is the elite of God's forces, designed by the Almighty to make men and women great at the art of Love and exceptional at the fine art of true Sex. And it would have never crossed my mind to introduce you to the League within the pages of this book had it not been for those twelve weeks of waiting.

In the panic over my inability to interview Great Sex, I scoured the countryside in order to find supporting evidence and sources willing to collaborate with me in making my case. The whole thing blew open approximately eleven weeks ago. I had received an anonymous tip about someone who might be willing to talk. When I checked out the source, nothing came of it.

Dejected, I was getting back into my car when I noticed a blue sticky note on my briefcase. Scrawled across its face were these words:

Great Sex may not talk, but there are others who can. Loodles Café—8:00 p.m.

The following chapters will recount for you the amazing and illuminating adventures that followed.

CHAPTER 4

The Wiry Little Guy

I arrived at my favorite local hangout, Cup of Loodles Café, punctually at eight o'clock. I found a table in the back of the establishment, figuring my newfound source might appreciate a bit of privacy.

"Well, if it ain't the Ludster!" greeted a friendly face, as he polished clean a tabletop five feet to the right of my chosen destination.

"Hey, Deuce." I smiled, a bit distracted.

"Can I get you the usual, Mr. Ludy?"

"Uh," I muttered, scanning the shop for any unknown characters. "Yeah, why don't you fix me up with the usual, but this time make it a large."

"One large hot chai, no frills, coming up."

I sat down at a small, round table near the hearth in the back. I hadn't even finished adjusting my notebook on the table when Deuce muttered my way again.

"By the way," he said with that drippy rag still in his hand, "that geeky dude over there wanted me to let you know he's waiting to meet with you."

I looked over toward the bookcase and saw a large, muscular man sitting snugly in a tall, wingback, leather chair only ten feet from where I sat.

"You mean the big guy?" I asked Deuce.

"No, the wiry little guy with big glasses and high-water pants, sitting right there. And beware, my friend, he's toting around a most awful smell."

Deuce was never one to mince words. When I shrugged my shoulders Deuce's way, letting him know I didn't see such a character in the café, he motioned again in the direction of the gargantuan man.

"The big guy?" I whispered, feeling extremely awkward with Deuce's continued use of a full-volume speaking voice, and somehow hoping against hope that my whispers would jar him into basic social etiquette.

Again, he pointed in the direction of the enormous man and stated, "No, the puny one!"

I got up from my chair, grabbing my notebook and pen, and waved dismissively at Deuce, figuring he was either playing with me or was seriously myopic. I walked up to the gigantic man, who was lost in a leather-bound book. I glanced at the book's spine and noticed with pleasant surprise that it was *The Scottish Chiefs*. "Are you enjoying the book?" I asked.

"It's a fine work, Mr. Ludy," he mused, looking up from behind his stylish glasses. "You once recommended it as a masterpiece, so I figured I would pick it up and see what type of literary connoisseur you actually are."

I noticed that he called me by name. "Are you the one who slipped me the note?"

"I am," he said plainly and confidently, turning his eyes back to the pages of the old book.

"I'm sorry, but have we met before?"

I stood awkwardly by his table as he read a few more sentences and then gently closed the book, set it on the table in front of him next to a half-empty mug of black coffee, and turned his eyes upward to look me dead-on.

"Actually, we know one another quite well, Mr. Ludy." A wry smile creased his face. "You've just never seen me before. But I have worked on your behalf for well over fifteen years now."

"Really?" I said, with a quizzical lift of the brow. "What's your name?"

"We'll get to that in due time, Mr. Ludy. First, why don't you sit down and get a little more comfortable."

The more I studied this man, the more familiar he seemed. His manner was reminiscent of something, but I just couldn't put my finger on it. He was hulking. His clothing covered it well, but as you looked at him more closely, it was obvious that this man was not just big; he seemed to be cut from marble with a Greek chisel. He was beyond Hollywood handsome, and his presence was truly statuesque and awesome. He smelled of Tide laundry detergent with a hint of peppermint. His jaw was square, his silvery-blue eyes were intense, and his grip, when he shook my hand, squashed my fingers.

"OK," I agreed, settling into a chair beside the man. "Just out of curiosity, did you ask Deuce—the man at the counter—to tell me that you were waiting for me?"

"I did."

"Why did he describe you as a wiry little guy in high-water pants?"

"Because to him, that is precisely what I am."

Deuce sees this massive, muscular man as a wiry little nerd? That didn't make sense. "What do you mean?"

"Mr. Ludy, let me explain something to you. You are one of the few people who sees me the way I actually am. I am not a mere person. I am quite different from you, different from that man behind the counter, and different from the rest of the people in this fine establishment. I am part of a very elite unit that has been around since the beginning of time. I am, in a sense, an agent of the Most High."

I paused for a moment, to let that sink in. *An agent of the Most High? Here? Having coffee with me?* "Sir, you said that we know each other well. But I'm having trouble remembering you. When did we meet?"

"In the winter months of 1990, you submitted your body to the rulership of the Almighty, and He immediately summoned me to begin my training in your inner life."

"But you can't tell me your name?"

"Again, we will get to that. For right now it is important that you listen closely and hold to what I'm about to tell you."

I leaned in with great expectation.

"I know you contacted Great Sex. That was a bold and brash move on your part. I realize you and Leslie have a special relationship with him in regard to your marriage; however, Great Sex is very private, and God has very strict authority over his public presentation. He called me into his office last week and told me you are writing a book that aims to prove his existence. I don't need to tell you how delicately this must be handled, Mr. Ludy!"

"I'm aware of the sacred nature of what I am bringing to light, sir, I assure you."

The gigantic man nodded grimly. "Well, Mr. Ludy, I expected Great Sex to decry your actions as subterfuge and dismiss them out of hand. However, much to my surprise, he asked me to help you. And within our prescribed bounds of modesty, decorum, and honor, he wants me to do what I can to assist you in bringing out the true identity of our sacred League."

"That's fantastic!" I smiled.

"Mr. Ludy," the man cautioned, "it will be fantastic only as far as you abide within my governance of the process."

"Absolutely. I will gladly submit to your authority as long as your authority stems from God Himself."

The hulk nodded his approval of my ready compliance.

I took the lid off my pen and flipped to a clean page in my notebook. "Let's get started, then. Could you tell me a little more about this 'League'?"

The man leaned back in his chair and took a sip of his coffee before answering. "I am one of four members of an elite band strategically put together by the Most High God. One of our duties is to protect and serve Great Sex."

"Who are the other three members?"

"You know them well, Mr. Ludy. You and your wife are two of our biggest advocates, which is why we are considering helping you with your book."

"Sorry to press you on this point, sir, but I'd really like to know your name."

"After I lay out one more ground rule."

"I'm listening."

"Whenever you speak or write on this subject, you must communicate that the League is never to become the focus of one's life. We are necessary operatives for any and all to reach the fullness of sexuality, but we must never detract from the real end-destination of a truly happy life, and that is Jesus Christ."

"I agree one hundred percent."

"Good." The large man leaned in closer and added, "Now may I ask you a question, Mr. Ludy?"

"Absolutely."

"You seemed to indicate in the first two chapters of your book that you actually know Great Sex personally."

"That's correct."

"Have you ever actually seen Great Sex?"

I thought about his question. *Had I ever seen Great Sex?* "Well, not exactly," I admitted. "I guess he's kind of like the wind. You know he is there. You experience his effect, but you can't just sit down across the table from him and chat."

"But you described him very specifically. For example, you mentioned that he has 'a hint of a British accent.'"

I could feel my cheeks getting warm. "Well, I'm sort of presuming he has a British accent."

"And he's 'William Wallace meets Lord Alfred Tennyson'?"

"Well, there again," I stammered, "even though we haven't actually had a formal chat, and I haven't actually studied all his features, I really think, from my own experience, that *is* what he is like."

"I see." The huge man grinned, seemingly enjoying my flustered answers to his interrogation. Then after a few awkward seconds, he said, "OK, then. So you haven't actually seen Great Sex, but you have experienced the benefits of his work, and you have surmised his personality from that experience."

"Exactly!" I agreed, happy that the man finally understood my ramblings.

The huge man relaxed his shoulders and sat back in his chair. A smile creased his face and a good-humored twinkle brightened his silver-blue eyes. It was at that moment that I unlocked the mystery of who he was.

"Is your name Mr. Purity?" I asked.

He seemed pleased that I finally remembered him. "It is indeed."

I grinned. "I thought I recognized you, but I've been struggling to put it all together."

Mr. Purity nodded and paused to take another sip of coffee. "As you well know, my name has fallen into a state of great reproach. And with this declining opinion of my importance, I have become increasingly unattractive to most people today."

I scribbled his words in my notebook as I continued the interview. "Are the other members of the League facing the same kind of misrepresentation?"

"It's shameful. We used to be synonymous with pleasure, and now we're lumped in with misery and sternness."

"You said I am well aware of the other three members of your elite band. Could you tell me their names?"

"Just as you figured out my name, you will figure out their names, Mr. Ludy. What is Great Sex, anyway, without mystery and adventure?"

I nodded, not fully appreciating this ambiguity. "Mr. Purity, you said in your note that you would be able to talk."

"Within reason, yes."

"Will the other members of the League also be willing to speak with me?"

"We are a supremely private group, Mr. Ludy. Let's take it one step at a time. If I sense that you are holding to the high standards of our holy coalition, then we can discuss additional interviews. You see, Mr. Ludy, I am the official bodyguard of the inner life. My responsibility is to protect the ever-maturing Christ-life within the hearts of God's children. And I also protect the innate and sacred beauty of the League. I am strong, and I can prove supremely stubborn when pressed. Yet if you heed to my way, young man, then I can assure you a great openness from the rest of my team."

"Fair enough."

"Mr. Ludy, I am a very congenial character once you get to know me. My business is to be cautious and guarded, but, as you have found in your own life, once you get past my brute exterior, you will see that I'm a pleasant chap."

I smiled knowingly and added, "I know from personal experience that when you are esteemed and your opinion heeded, great things follow. You are the best at what you do, Mr. Purity, and your team is definitely safe with you as their front man. So, just as I've done in my private life, I will seek to honor you in what I am writing."

"Well, now that we've gotten the business out of the way, I have some thoughts I would like to share with you that I believe will help you immensely."

I flipped to a clean page on my notepad and poised my pen over the page.

At this moment, Deuce arrived at our table bearing a large ceramic mug full of steaming hot chai. "Here you go, Ludster. Sorry it took me so long. I got hit with a steady stream of customers right after you ordered."

"Thanks," I said, smiling up at Deuce.

As Deuce turned to leave, I said, "Hey Deuce, would you mind being bluntly honest with me?"

"Am I ever not bluntly honest?" he chuckled.

I gestured toward Mr. Purity. "You see this man I'm talking with?"

"Yeah," Deuce said with a tinge of disgust in his voice.

"How tall do you think he is?"

"What?"

"I know it's a strange question, but I'm really interested in your perspective."

"Oh, I don't know," Deuce said, studying the man in front of him. "Maybe five feet, five-foot-two. Somewhere in there."

I nodded. "Why do you think I am meeting with him?"

"Uh, how would I know?" Deuce shifted his feet uncomfortably.

"Come on, Deuce. I just want you to be bluntly honest and tell me why you think I am sitting here talking with this man."

"Well, you are all into that Christian stuff, and it's probably your job to meet with people like this, you know, people who need help and all that. It's probably one of those rules you're forced to obey from the Bible."

"Thank you, Deuce, your answers have been most illuminating."

"No offense, mister," Deuce said, looking down at the man in front of him, "but he asked me to be honest."

"No offense taken," responded Purity with a kind smile. "I get that rather often."

"Well, you might consider a shower and shave once in a

while. You might not be all that bad if you just put a little work into your, you know, your grooming habits."

"A most excellent idea," smiled Purity.

"Thank you, Deuce." I smiled, hinting with my tone that his blunt honesty could come to an end.

"Anytime!" Deuce shouted as he headed back to his work duties.

With my tall chai in front of me, my pen in hand, and my notepad before me, I explored a new dimension in my relationship with Mr. Purity. As we talked, I was forced to admit that there was a time I, too, would have seen this hulking hero as a runty, nerdy sort of fellow. However, as I listened to him, I witnessed as if for the very first time the majesty in his voice, the nobility in his cadence, and the passion in his every manner. Once again I was awed by the strength of Purity. I longed for even more of his grandeur and moral presence in my life.

In the next chapter, I will attempt to detail the highlights from our enlightening conversation.

CHAPTER 5

The Deal

The way I see it, Mr. Ludy," Mr. Purity said, "you have your work cut out for you in writing this book."

"Do you think it's possible," I asked, "to make an airtight case for Great Sex?"

Purity paused. "I'll be straight with you, young man. Great Sex is real; we both know that. But unless people actually experience this extraordinary pleasure firsthand, there will remain reasons to doubt his authenticity. And these reasons, no matter how ignorant and uninformed they seem to you and me, can certainly serve as fuel for the opposition and thusly impair the tightness of your case."

"But isn't there another way to make the case?" I questioned. "After all, when juries hear a case in court, they are presented with evidence that demonstrates the truth of something none of them personally witnessed."

"That is true, Mr. Ludy, but here is the difference. No one who has truly ever witnessed the grandeur of Great Sex is allowed to speak of it in intimate detail, without violating one of the cardinal rules that make Great Sex *great* in the first place, and that is modesty, decorum, nobility, and cherished secrecy. You've been assuming that Great Sex would blab just like Imposter Sex, but such indiscretion is altogether outside his nature."

"You're right," I admitted, as my heart plummeted. I felt an all-too-familiar ache begin nibbling at my insides. It's the ache that comes with being an author, when you finally face up to the fact that your connections have fallen through and your research is unattainable.

"It's impossible!" I croaked in sudden despair. "I can't possibly expose Imposter Sex and introduce Great Sex without violating the noble code of conduct that makes Great Sex great."

"Come on, Mr. Ludy! Show some fight!" barked Mr. Purity. "I'm not saying your project is without merit; I'm only saying you have your work cut out for you. You are going to need an avant-garde approach. And this is precisely why Great Sex asked me to assist you. He thinks you have a shot at making a difference with your book, but he's certain that you can't do it without our help."

"So how would you propose to help me? Can you get me an interview with Great Sex?"

The man chuckled good-naturedly. "Mr. Ludy, the odds are greater for you to squeeze a pregnant hippo into your shirt pocket than for me to squeeze an interview out of Great Sex."

I winced at the word picture. "Then what kind of evidence can I use to make my argument?"

Mr. Purity set his coffee mug on the table and leaned in. "Mr. Ludy, consider the possibility that people may not be looking for circumstantial evidence. Maybe they simply need to hear from you that Great Sex is real. I myself am a close associate with Great Sex—*use me*. I have insider knowledge of the whole Great Sex process, as do my colleagues. If you prove to me that you respect the necessary purity of this proposed project, then I can guarantee you that your audience will have more than their fill of evidence, even if they haven't personally experienced Great Sex."

I took a moment to reflect on what Purity was saying. Then after a long pause, I nodded in agreement and said, "All right, let's go for it."

"OK, then."

"So what can you tell me that can really help my audience?" I clicked the end of my pen in anticipation.

"Mr. Ludy, remember the course God brought you through back in 1994, when you married Leslie, entitled Finding Great Sex 101?"

"Sure."

"Well, I was the professor who taught the course."

I paused a moment while I studied his features, trying to find something that would help me remember him. "That was *you*?"

"It is obvious, Mr. Ludy, that even though we have worked together since early 1990, there are a few things of which you are still quite ignorant."

"Please don't take offense at this, Mr. Purity, but it surprises me that you are so connected with Great Sex. When I think about it, it makes total sense, but I guess I've subconsciously disassociated purity from the pleasure dimension of God's kingdom. You always seemed so serious, so frigid; I assumed you never even thought about things like Sex."

Purity laughed uproariously. "I see you still have some remaining false notions about Sex floating around in that head of yours, Mr. Ludy. Great Sex and Purity are inseparable, like two peas in a pod."

"It's funny how those thoughts get ingrained," I said.

"Well, if it's any consolation, the idea that I'm serious, uptight, and frigid is a very popular notion. The truth be told, I'm just as exciting as Great Sex when you get to know me. The excitement I offer is full of adventure and mystery. I, my young friend, specialize in the thrill of triumph and the pleasures of liberty!"

"Yeah, I can see that now. And it is clear to me how you have brought those things to my life."

"So getting back to your question regarding what I can tell you that could help your readers—I can give you what no one else can: I can tell you all about Great Sex. Whereas, there are those like yourself who know him for his artistry, I know him personally, Mr. Ludy. In fact, I know his every passion and his every pet peeve."

"And you would be willing to share these things?"

"That depends entirely upon you, my friend. As far as you respect me and follow my lead, to that same degree will I entrust to you these secrets over time."

I couldn't help feeling a twinge of disappointment. "Over time? Does that mean you won't share these things with me tonight?"

"Mr. Ludy, I am a man who delights in mystery. What would I do to my reputation if I divulged every secret I possess all at once?"

I bit my lower lip with concern over this development.

Thoughts of book deadlines danced like sugar plums in my head. "Oh, OK. So what *can* you share with me tonight?"

"Mr. Ludy, I would like to make you a deal."

"What kind of deal?"

"You allow me to test you over these next four weeks, to prove you like I've never done before, and then I will consider letting you in on a few of my secrets."

I was skeptical. "Why do you need to test me? Haven't you already done that?"

"My work in the domain of the heart is never complete. I must continually pull away new layers of self in order to make room for more of Christ."

"So why do you need to test me before you can speak to me?"

"Because in God's kingdom, the messengers of truth must not be hypocrites. The truth must be true to them, authenticated in their lives; otherwise, you end up with messengers who say things that are true but live lies."

I swallowed hard. I had no idea what Mr. Purity meant by "prove me like never before," but I found myself extending my hand toward him and sealing the deal. After all, what other options did I have? This guy was my only lead.

"I'm in," I said.

"Four weeks from now, Mr. Ludy. Same time, same place."

"How can I reach you before then if I need you?"

"Trust me, Mr. Ludy. You will soon realize that I shadow your every movement. God is jealous over your life, and I, my friend, am His personal expression of that love. So I will always be close, but my work over these next four weeks will be done in silence."

"So we can't talk until then?"

"It will be far more important that you talk with God during these next twenty-eight days, rather than with me."

And with that mysterious statement, our conversation ended—and the four weeks of testing began.

CHAPTER 6

Purity Test

If someone asked me if I know Harold Bloom, the school-teacher, I could say, "Certainly," and not be telling a falsehood. But in reality, exchanging names, shaking the man's hand, and jabbering for three minutes about the weather doesn't quite add up to the idea of "knowing" someone.

When I started writing this book, I thought I knew Purity. And I was quite certain that I knew Great Sex. And while I did know the two of them in a sense, the way I know Purity and Sex *now*, as a result of writing this book, makes it almost seem like my previous relationship with them involved nothing more than exchanging names, shaking hands, and jabbering for three minutes about the weather.

But that's just the pattern of growth in God's kingdom. With every step forward, we look back at ourselves in dismay at how obvious and enormous God is and how little credit or room to maneuver we actually gave Him.

I'm going to be honest with you. This book wasn't supposed to be a challenge. Leslie and I have written multiple books and spoken internationally on issues pertaining to sex for the past twelve years. I should be able to do an exposé on this subject with one arm tied behind my back, a 1943 typewriter, and a single bottle of whiteout. After all, I am very well acquainted with the work of Great Sex and I am a huge fan of his artistic abilities. This book should have been a walk in the park.

But as I allowed God to test me, prove me, and shine His searchlight into my soul, I realized how much more there was to Purity and Great Sex than I'd ever known.

When Mr. Purity proposed a test, I jutted out my hand and shook on it. But this test was deeper, more penetrating, and far more acute than anything I had previously known.

If you don't mind, I would like to take you back in time a few weeks in order to familiarize you with certain events that transpired in Leslie's and my life that set the stage for this test to become so extra special.

You see, the day I was preparing to leave for New York to interview Imposter Sex (as chronicled in chapter 1), Leslie announced to me that she was pregnant with our second child. I thought the timing seemed marvelously ideal.

"Beef," she had written in a love note. "It's actually happened! We are going to be parents again!"

With a smile in my soul, I headed out to New York for the showdown with Imposter Sex, confident that I wasn't just a fanatic aficionado of Great Sex, but I was once again privileged to enjoy the fruit of his bounty. I must admit, it gave me an extra kick in my step for the journey.

I arrived back from New York, very pleased with the way the

interview had gone, and everything was blissfully wonderful in our lives. Leslie and I were dreaming of life with our yet-unborn addition, planning baby-room design themes, and even strategizing travel plans for the upcoming year, knowing that this pregnancy was going to alter a few things.

It was about four weeks into this bliss that Leslie and I were thunderstruck with terrible news. It was the very same day I placed the first two chapters of this manuscript into the hands of Great Sex's agent and begged him to have Great Sex read it. When I returned home later that day, I saw Leslie waiting for me in the doorway with tears in her eyes.

"What's wrong, Love?" I asked gently as I stepped out of the car.

She had trouble speaking, and moments later I found myself holding her sobbing body in my arms as she shared with me the devastating news: our unborn child had died. Leslie had miscarried.

Anyone who has gone through a miscarriage knows how difficult it is. It's a loss. And any loss of human life, no matter how small the life is, is hard. But as uncomfortable as this news was, and as difficult as it has proved in our lives, I must admit that God somehow turned this tragedy into a triumph. For it was about a week later that I found the blue sticky note from Mr. Purity on my briefcase. So in this state of heart-tenderness, God gave my soul the medicine I needed most. He gave me the Purity Test.

It's amazing how trials and disappointments can cause us to become spiritually sensitive, force us to our knees, and open us up to a new and deeper work of God in our hearts. Mr. Purity entered in at a time when I was hurting, and though his work was painful, it was also what ultimately healed me.

In addition to the miscarriage of our unborn child, there had been a series of other miscarriages in my soul that I wasn't even aware of. God, using the strong arm of Purity, was helping me to see four distinct things.

First, I realized that diligent, heartfelt, and Spirit-born prayer had miscarried in my soul, leaving only a trickle of unimpassioned, human-derived prayers. Prayer had been relegated to available slots within my day and had lost its once vibrant presence in my daily life. I used to pray with passion, with purpose, and with expectancy; now I prayed to maintain, to pacify, and to keep the Flesh in check. I had lost a treasure, and I was distraught to discover that I hadn't even realized it was gone.

Second, my absolute and childlike confidence in God and His Word had also miscarried in my soul. Sure, I knew that God was capable of great and powerful things, but no longer was I proving with my every attitude and action that He was almighty and all-powerful. I was living as if a big God was out there somewhere, but not as if that big God was actually operating my existence. My faith was active, but no longer living and stoked with a child's Christmas morning expectancy. I had lost a treasure, and again, like prayer, I hadn't even realized it was gone.

Third, I had forgotten the first loves God had stirred in my heart. Leslie and I fell in love while talking about reaching the poor, the orphan, the widow, the lonely, the foreigner, the least among the crowds—this had been our passion, our purpose, to carry Christ's love, His grace, His good news to such as these. But what had started as a pure desire for service had turned into the machine of ministry. My thoughts were on paying bills, preparing messages, setting up logistics, discipling leaders, and a hundred other seemingly important things. But somehow amid this pressing business of the "kingdom of God," I had forgotten the ones who make up the kingdom of God. I had forgotten the little ones, the foolish ones, the disabled ones, the ones in desperate need of an advocate. The loss of our unborn child, as hard as it was, reminded me that the weak and helpless ones are the ones Christ remembers. I had miscarried those pure longings that had been conceived in the innocence of childlike surrender and trust.

Fourth, I realized that I wasn't submitted to God in some of the most important areas of my life, and this realization horrified me. The very thing I had detested most about modern Christian leaders when I started out in ministry I suddenly realized had become a part of my life. I was outraged—as a twenty-one-year-old man of fiery zeal—that Christian leaders could allow their lives to disconnect from their messages. I remember saying to Leslie several years ago, "How is it possible to talk about Jesus all day long and not realize that your life isn't matching up?" But there I was, standing before the bright light of Purity, exposed as a sham. I talked about abandoning to God, trusting God in every situation, but was I? I had convinced myself that since I talked about it so much it must be real within me. Yet, in fact, so much of my life had come back under *my* control. I was the one living my life; it wasn't Christ living my life. And I was asking Christ to bless *my* decisions, *my* dictation of how I felt my life could best represent Him. I found myself broken and humbled, yet amazed at how gently Purity expressed to me the love and mercy of God in doing His housecleaning.

Whenever we allow Purity to do his work within our hearts, it appears at the outset that the process will be grim and miserable. However, the work of Purity actually breeds the opposite effect. Purity brings freedom, life, love, and a sense of stability and fortification for which every human heart longs. Purity uses his strong arm to wrench out the darkest and most awful junk of the human soul. But the reason he removes this junk isn't to create a gigantic junk-shaped hole in our lives; rather, he fills the hole with the treasures of Jesus Christ and the fullness of His life and love.

I know it may seem odd that I have interjected this chapter into this story about Great Sex. After all, what does my personal encounter with Purity have to do with your personal encounter with Great Sex?

It has everything to do with it.

Here's a basic, simple, oft-overlooked truth about Great Sex: to the degree we allow Purity to work in our souls, God will allow us to understand and appreciate Great Sex.

Purity is the one who trains and grooms us for Great Sex. If we allow him to test us, prove us, and shape us—we are molded into one worthy of the King's very best. As a result of Purity's recent work in my heart and soul, Leslie and I have experienced a deeper relationship with the King of all kings, as well as a whole new level of beauty, romance, intimacy, and delight in our love relationship. To the degree we allow Mr. Purity to have his way, we discover the amazing fullness of the life God designed for His children.

A Step Further

In the back of this book, Leslie and I have included some content to help you practically implement these truths into your life.

You may be at a completely different place in your life than I was during my purity test. You may not be married, and you may not be working through the loss of an unborn child. But no matter what your particular life situation, in order to begin your journey to discover Great Sex, you must first allow Purity to have his way in your life.

In appendix A, we have included a purity test you can customize in your own life. We placed this information in the back of the book instead of right here in the middle of the story to give you the option of when and how you experience the process of practical, personal application. If you are ready to dig deeper on this point of Purity, then flip forward to appendix A and start digging. However, if you are in the flow of the book and wish to save the digging for later, then continue on with chapter 7 and enjoy.

CHAPTER 7

A Hundred Little Puppy Dogs

Four weeks is typically a long time to wait for a follow-up interview, but in this situation, I began to realize that Purity, though he wasn't giving me quotable sound bites, was teaching me extraordinary things and introducing me to profound new ideas. Sure they were four long weeks, but they were four of the most important weeks of my life. Mr. Purity is an amazing teacher, and even though I had seemingly known him quite well for nearly two decades, I realized through this twenty-eight-day test that he was a much more significant player in this great drama of life than I had previously thought.

If you didn't know better, you might think that Mr. Purity is the low man on the League's totem pole. But meeting Mr. Purity helped me understand that he is the strongest and possibly the most complete and extraordinary member of the entire bunch, because he's the one who gives muscle to the rest of these extraordinary heroes. He's the Secret Service, the bodyguard, the frontline defense for the entire superhero outfit. He's pure strength, nobility, and honor. Without him, there is no League. Without him, there is no Great Sex.

In other words, how we handle Purity defines our entire course. If we snub him, we snub not only the rest of the League and Great Sex, but we are snubbing Jesus Christ, who commissioned Mr. Purity to prepare our souls for more and more of His love and life.

When the four weeks had completed, I found myself a stronger man, and what had started out merely as a book project had turned into a life adventure. I was bursting with fascination to see what lay ahead. After giving Leslie a quick kiss good-bye, I gathered my keys, pen, and notepad, and I hopped into my car.

I pulled into the parking lot outside of Cup of Loodles Café and found myself eager with anticipation. It was obvious that God was doing something in my life, and He was doing something in and through this book project. What would happen next?

"It's the Ludster!" greeted Deuce with his patented enthusiasm as I meandered in through the jangling front door. "Can I get you the usual?"

"I'd appreciate that, Deuce!" I answered with a smile. "But this time, make it an extra-large with a squirt of whip."

Deuce smiled, appreciating the fact that I was adding some pizzazz to my ever-predictable rut. Looking around the café, I didn't see Mr. Purity anywhere. And believe me, he's difficult to miss. I walked to the back table, peering around the large mahogany bookshelves—there was no one there. My heart sank. I looked at my watch. Sure enough, it was 8:01. It wasn't like a member of the League to be late.

I turned back toward Deuce, who seemed to anticipate my question. "Over there," he said with a smirk. "Another one of your pitiful ministry projects."

I looked in the direction Deuce was pointing and saw an attractive young woman.

"Thanks," I said, a bit confused. Once again, what Deuce was seeing as pitiful was anything but. This young woman literally gleamed with joy. Her eyes twinkled, and her cheeks were rosy with childlike anticipation. She was stunning yet not in the way that word would be typically used. She possessed a pure, flowerlike loveliness and was beyond beautiful. In fact, the word *beautiful* would be almost condescending to what she possessed. She had a royal presence and an air of mystery. If she had makeup on I didn't notice it, for her smile jumped from her face like a hundred little puppy dogs, attracting all my attention.

"Peeps!" she said in a sweet voice. She seemed to be addressing me.

"Uh, hello, ma'am," I stammered, attempting to gain my bearings. "Do I know you?"

"Of course, you know me, silly," she said with a laugh. "You've just never seen me in this form." She pushed back her chair and rose to her feet, extending her delicate fingers to politely shake my hand.

She was full of an unusual, even extraordinary, childlike energy and excitement, but seemed to be governed by a mystical dignity and composure. It was as if those hundred little puppy dogs were longing to leap from her being and lick my face, but a massive leather chain held them back and forced them to heel at her side.

"I must forewarn you, dear friend," she said with a wide grin,

"Mr. Purity is standing only ten feet away, and he is watching your every move to see if you are worthy to interview me."

I looked over my shoulder. Sure enough, there Mr. Purity stood, camouflaged by a tall plastic myrtle tree, observing me carefully. I swallowed hard.

"Don't worry, Peeps," she counseled. "He won't bother you as long as you respect me."

"Why do you keep calling me Peeps?" I asked.

"It's my nickname for you!" she announced playfully. "I've called you that since you were seventeen. When you laugh, you open your mouth and I fully expect a loud roar of hilarity to issue forth; however, absolutely no sound comes out. It is truly entertaining to watch. You slap your leg, turn red in the face, hold your stomach, and still not a sound comes out. And then, finally, little squeaks of laughter come out. I call those little squeaks of laughter 'peeps,' and I cherish them, for they remind me of the joy of Jesus."

I was surprised that she seemed to know me so intimately. "Um . . . can I ask what *your* name is?"

She shook her head good-naturedly. "Mr. Purity told me you would ask that question."

"He knows me well," I smiled.

"Considering your previous dealings with our friend, Mr. Purity, I'm sure you will not be surprised to hear that he has requested I not divulge my name to you. He is convinced that the mystery will make the process more meaningful and fun. And I must agree. So, dear one, I guess you are going to have to figure it out."

I sighed. "Everything is so mysterious with you all."

"It's very purposeful, I assure you. You see, *patience* and *discovery* are two of the most delightful elements to God's great kingdom life. If you were given everything you ask for when you ask for it, and if waiting and exploration were not a part of the journey, then you would never fully appreciate the discovery when you attain it." Her eyes twinkled knowingly. "It's a lot like the process you went through back in 1990, when you submitted your whole life to Christ."

"When I started this journey, I didn't expect to be thrust back in time to my premarriage days. Why do you and Mr. Purity keep referring to what I went through back then?"

"That's a very astute observation, Peeps," she said. "You see, you have chosen to write a book about Great Sex. But Great Sex is not merely found once. It is meant to be discovered a hundred, even a thousand, times throughout a lifetime. And every time it is found, it is found by the exact same means—an increased familiarity with Jesus Christ and His League. And every time Great Sex is discovered, he is discovered in a fuller more beautiful way. And I believe it is safe to say that never has Great Sex been discovered to his fullest measure by any living soul."

She looked at me with empathy and then continued, "My dearest Peeps. You began this book project thinking you had already discovered Great Sex and were ready to show him to the world, but you had merely discovered Great Sex at a beginner's level."

I was embarrassed by her accusation and felt my face turning four shades of red. "Only at a beginner's level?" I mumbled.

She nodded and grinned, amused by my awkwardness. "But I'm happy to say, my dear Peeps, that there is hope for you."

The two of us were still standing. She pointed to a seat across from her chair and motioned for me to sit down.

"Thank you," I said, maneuvering toward my seat.

"Now, Mr. Ludy, I'm certain I've taught you better manners than that!" She had her hands upon her hips and a disapproving expression.

"Oh, please forgive me," I said, realizing that she was waiting for me, as a noble gentleman, to help her to her seat before claiming my own. Which, after being publicly derided for my oversight, I proceeded to do with cheeks flaming in embarrassment.

"Thank you, kind sir," she said graciously and then smiled at me.

"My pleasure." I grinned back, as she took her seat.

As I ventured around the table and settled into my own seat, the familiar hulking figure of Mr. Purity appeared beside us. He was still watching me carefully, but his expression was much more relaxed than before.

"So did I pass the test?" I asked Mr. Purity as he pulled up a chair to join us.

"Just barely," said Purity, letting a grin slip through his lips.

"Don't let him fool you," said the young woman. "He was bragging about you just last night at our weekly League meeting."

"Hush, girl!" Purity teased. "What happens at our meetings stays at our meetings. I don't want this guy thinking I'm some softie."

"Peeps," she added, "he thinks you are ready to meet the League."

I looked at Purity to verify this bit of amazing information.

Purity gave a knowing look to the young woman and then allowed a large smile to fill his chiseled face. "I must admit," he said, "you've surprised me, Mr. Ludy. You didn't shy away when I turned up the heat. You took seriously every little thing I poked at in your soul. You allowed me to take you to an entirely new level of cleanliness. I believe you really want it."

"I do. I really do!" I assured him.

Purity looked at the young woman, and she nodded her approval. Then Purity turned back toward me. "All right. You've made it through phase one. I'll give you interview access to the other three members of our League."

"What about Great Sex? Can you get me in with him?"

"You've only made it through phase one, young man," he cautioned. "You prove faithful with them, and then we will discuss the vast improbability of your actually interviewing Great Sex."

"Fair enough," I said. I didn't want to lose anything I had just gained by upsetting Mr. Purity.

"All right then," Purity began in a businesslike tone, "here are our terms. We will provide you with four interviews. If you prove yourself loyal, discreet, loving, and honorable in how you handle yourself, then we will open up additional discussions. Each of the interviews will be on our terms and not yours. They will be held in locations of our choosing, at times that we deem most favorable. Agreed?"

"Agreed."

"And you must clearly communicate in your book that Great Sex and the League will become useless, impotent, and weak the moment that they themselves become the focus rather than Jesus Christ. Life isn't about Purity, and it is unequivocally not about Great Sex. Life is about Jesus Christ, and if He is given His rightful place in a person's life, then Great Sex, Purity, and the rest of the League are able to work their magic. Understood?"

"Understood."

"OK, then."

"Does that mean you are ready to talk?"

"It does."

"Great! So can I interview both of you right now?"

"You will interview only me at this time, Mr. Ludy," said Mr. Purity. "I brought this attractive woman along merely as a means of determining your readiness." He turned to the woman and winked at her. "Besides, Mr. Ludy, if you think *I* hold high standards, just wait till you get a load of this girl!"

They both chuckled. After taking a sip of her tea, she turned to me and said, "Peeps, after witnessing your willingness and readiness to conform to the pattern of Christ, I'm prepared to give my endorsement as well."

"Thank you so much!" I blurted enthusiastically.

The young woman leaned across the table and said, "It was *his* idea, I hope you know." She pointed at her muscular attendant.

"His idea for what?" I asked.

"Oh, to tell you to take a seat," she answered, "and then chide you for your poor manners when you didn't pull out my chair. He went on and on about it the entire way over here, begging me to do it." She smiled widely.

Mr. Purity laughed. "Yeah, that was good. But the best one was the line about your being at the beginner's level in regard to Great Sex. A sublime truth, I might add. That was a classic moment. You should have seen your face." He mimicked my strained and awkward expression and burst out with uproarious laughter.

I watched the two of them laugh and found myself joining in. The Beauty and the Beef. She was delicate and mysterious;

he was strong and forthright. Strangely enough, I did know both of them quite well. And as they laughed, I realized that I had laughed with them many times before. And it was at that moment that I realized who she was.

She was Sacred.

My wife called her Set Apart, and throughout Christian history she had been known as Holiness. But no matter the name, this was she all right. The eyes, the rosy cheeks, the laughter, that veil of mystery, the smile that grips your heart like a hundred pouncing puppy dogs—this was definitely Sacred. And wow! She was simply breathtaking.

"You know who I am now, don't you?" she said with a twinkle in her eye.

"Yeah, I do. I'm surprised I didn't see it right away."

I realized Mr. Purity and Sacred were holding hands. "Are you two . . . uh . . ." I stopped, not quite knowing how you ask two superheroes if they are a couple.

"Since the beginning," Mr. Purity affirmed. "We have always been inseparable."

I reached for my pen and notepad. Whether the interview had officially started or not, I wanted to remember all of this.

"I'm the reason this guy even knows how to laugh," Sacred said. "I'm scared to think what would become of him if he didn't have me."

"Well," mumbled Mr. Purity, "you wouldn't be doing so hot without me, now would you, dear?" He leaned over and gave her a quick kiss.

I watched this interchange between Purity and Sacred and couldn't help but shake my head in wonder. I didn't know one person on planet earth who would guess that these two knew how to laugh and have fun. But here they were, kissing and grinning ear to ear as if that were completely normal behavior for them.

Everything was beginning to make sense. Purity and Holiness need each other. Purity is the power of God to clean and protect our inner house from unwanted invaders, while Holiness is the power of God to make our inner life beautiful and fragrant and enjoyable.

Without Sacred, Purity would become Puritanism—a dour, brittle revolt against pleasure, fun, laughter, beauty, and all things sweet. And without Purity, Holiness would become "Holier than Thou"—a proud, pompous presentation of our finest attempts at looking like we are spiritually strong, when in actuality we are spiritually weak.

Purity humbles. Sacred makes lovely. Purity fights. Sacred surrenders. Purity snarls at the enemy. Sacred embraces the Victor. Purity issues a war cry. Sacred sings a love song. Purity eliminates. Sacred replenishes. Purity cleans. Sacred furnishes. Purity is muscle. Sacred is shapeliness. Purity balances the checkbook. Sacred spends on the things that are most important.

I found myself jotting down all these thoughts. I must have grown oblivious to the world about me, for, to my consternation, when I looked up, the two of them were gone. A blue sticky note on the table read:

Let's do it again. Tomorrow morning, 5:30. Loodles Cafe.

"Five thirty?" I mouthed with horror. Then realizing who had penned the note, I smiled and let out a hearty chuckle.

Meet Mr. Smith

CHAPTER 8

A Soul in the Stew

I did a strange thing.

You see, before I left Loodles last night after my brief encounter with Sacred and Mr. Purity, I asked Deuce if he would meet with me at five o'clock the following morning, before I met with Mr. Purity. I knew Deuce was opening up the café the next day, so I gave it a whirl. He had always found me a bit fascinating, so he agreed to my odd proposal. But, whereas you might consider my invitation to Deuce strange, that wasn't the strange thing that I did.

The following morning at five o'clock, I arrived at the café with sleep in my eyes and an interesting hankering in my soul.

"Hey, Ludster!" Deuce greeted with a little less volume and enthusiasm than usual.

"Good morning, Deuce," I offered back.

He whipped me up a hot chai and brewed himself a mocha

latte. We sat down at a table near the mahogany bookshelves and Deuce asked, "So what's up?"

Now here is where I did the strange thing. I whipped out my manuscript, everything I had written so far, and laid it in front of Deuce.

"What's this?" he asked with amusement.

"It's a book I'm writing."

"You're trying to write a book?"

"I know—it's bewildering, isn't it?" I smiled. I placed my hand on the manuscript and said, "Would you mind reading this for me? I'm fascinated to see what you think. Oh, and by the way"—I smiled mysteriously—"you're in it!"

I sipped my chai with great anticipation as Deuce turned the pages. He laughed a couple of times, and I attempted to see what part of the manuscript he was reading, but my angle was poorly chosen, and I could only guess as to where he actually was. At one point he snickered and rolled his eyes, and I thought, *Hmm, not exactly what I am after.* But overall, he seemed to be enjoying himself. Excluding his comment about how I should pick a subject a little more in my league and the fact that I misquoted him on page 33, my guess is that he actually liked it.

Here's the weird part. While he was reading, Mr. Purity came in through the jangling door. Deuce didn't even notice. The big guy strolled up alongside our table and nodded at me, casting a questioning gaze toward the young man sitting across from me.

"Just a little test marketing," I said.

Mr. Purity smiled knowingly, reached into his satchel, pulled out his copy of *The Scottish Chiefs*, and found himself a warm spot near the hearth to read the further adventures of William Wallace.

Deuce didn't even know he was there. And it wasn't until he had made his snide remark about the inappropriateness of my writing on the subject of Great Sex that he caught wind of Purity sitting only ten feet behind him.

"Dear God," he exclaimed, turning white as a sheet, "it's you!"

"Yes, it's me all right," said Mr. Purity calmly.

"How long have you been here?" asked Deuce.

"Oh, I've been hovering over your shoulder now for, oh, I'd say, twenty-two, going on twenty-three years now, Mr. Johnson. Does that sound about right to you?"

Deuce just stared back at him with a pale face.

"What's wrong, Deuce?" I asked, puzzled by my friend's bizarre behavior.

Deuce muttered something under his breath that sounded akin to cursing and then looked back at me and said, "Why'd you make me read this? I was fine! My life was fine! Now I'm seeing what you are seeing!"

He slammed down the manuscript and got up from the table. He didn't talk to me the rest of the morning.

"That's strange," I muttered to myself.

"No," said Mr. Purity strolling over to the table and pulling up his chair. "It's not strange at all."

"You're telling me that wasn't strange?"

"Your friend Deuce is not responding to you, me, or even to your manuscript, Mr. Ludy—he's responding to the conviction of Christ upon his soul. When he recognized me, his soul was attuning itself to the fact that what you have written is all true. And, Mr. Ludy, you must realize that if what you have written is all true, then Deuce is realizing right now that he is all false."

I have thought about Mr. Purity's statement about Deuce quite a bit since that morning. I think I take for granted that Mr. Purity and Sacred are actually real characters, bona fide personalities desiring to take a chisel to our lives. But I can understand how strange it might sound if you'd never thought of them as anything but mythical ideals generated by pious religious folk to create a false sense of moral constraint. When I actually think about it, the book I'm writing may seem bizarre to some of you out there. Whereas Great Sex is something you wouldn't mind learning a little about, the idea of Purity and Sacred is not a glamorous one. In fact, it sounds a bit like dry grits and overcooked eggs for breakfast.

"I was sort of hoping," I said to Mr. Purity as he sat down in his chair, "that I could ask Deuce a few questions about his thoughts. But thanks to you—"

"Thanks to me," interrupted Mr. Purity, "that young man is now forced to deal with the fact that what you are writing is true." He paused. "And Jimmy the Shrimp is not going to release his control over Deuce without a fight."

I thought about that for a second. It was true. That explained Deuce's strong reaction to reading the manuscript. Deuce was still under the control of Jimmy the Shrimp's regime, so he recoiled when he saw Mr. Purity and Sacred as their true selves, evidenced in the lives of God's people.

"You sure do have a way of making people uncomfortable," I told Mr. Purity.

"Yes," he responded with a shrug, "but that's merely the kingdom pattern for stirring souls. I'm a pot stirrer, Mr. Ludy. When people see me or my handiwork in you, they are confronted with how far away they really are from reflecting Jesus Christ."

"Conviction," I said knowingly.

"Conviction," Mr. Purity repeated in agreement.

"How does that differ from condemnation?"

"They are worlds apart, my friend. Conviction is a work of love and hope, the gentle touch of truth upon the heart, mind, and soul to allow a person to see that he stands upon a precipice and must turn and walk a new way." Mr. Purity leaned in and grew very serious. "Condemnation is of a completely different family tree. It's the state of a person who refuses the rescuing hand of Christ. *Conviction* is what saves a misguided person from *condemnation*."

"I like that," I said. "Conviction is what saves a misguided person from condemnation."

"It gives a whole new meaning to your statement, 'But thanks to you,' doesn't it?"

The two of us laughed.

"So what's happening in Deuce right now?" I asked.

Mr. Purity glanced at Deuce, who was busy serving morning customers at the front counter. "I'd say he's feeling a sting upon his soul, an unfamiliar pressure upon his heart."

"How will he respond?"

"That's between Deuce and the Spirit of God, Mr. Ludy. But one thing is for sure. Deuce has been forced to reckon with God. And that means a soul in the stew."

"What does that mean?"

"Oh, 'a soul in the stew' is how we describe a life in the stew pot of conviction, in which the water gets increasingly hotter and hotter. That soul either finally jumps out of the boiling misery into the arms of grace—or it cooks in its own juices."

"That's disgusting!" I grimaced.

"I fully agree, Mr. Ludy. And that is why when a soul is in the stew, you must pray for it as if eternity hangs in the balance—for it does."

So, long and short, I did a strange thing this morning. I handed my unfinished manuscript to Deuce Johnson, and now his soul is "in the stew."

The purpose of this book isn't to throw people into the stew-pot of conviction; however, time spent in the stew usually translates into the most profound bliss not long after. So if you find yourself getting a bit feverish with conviction as you read this book, allow those hot waters to do you a favor and push you into the open arms of Christ's sweet grace. After all, when the garbage in our soul is exposed, it doesn't feel very good at first. But the reason it is exposed is so that it can be cleaned. This is what Mr. Purity specializes in—illuminating junk in the soul, removing junk from the soul, and keeping junk out of the soul from then on. It's painful, yes. But the end result of such a soul procedure is transcendent joy and peace.

"So," I said to Mr. Purity, "are you ready to begin our first official interview?"

"I am," the big man answered with a grin.

"Well," I said, pulling out my pen and notepad. "Let's get started."

The odd thing about my interview with Mr. Purity, as you will find out for yourself in the upcoming chapter, is that it was inordinately short but extraordinarily profound. Maybe that is a truth about Purity in and of itself. His work isn't meant to be arduously long but rather, simple, to the point, and supremely effective. He doesn't want us in "the stew" any longer than is necessary. If he had his way, we would all say to Christ, "Do it, Lord! Try me, test me, purge me, remake me!" And then Purity would simply do his job and move us forward. He's that sort of a guy. And to tell you the truth, I like that quality a lot.

Sure, Purity's job is never done in the human soul, but that doesn't mean we are supposed to live in the stew pot. Mr. Purity does his work so that we can live in the most satisfying, fulfilling, heaven-come-to-earth embrace of our precious Jesus. The stew pot may be necessary to awaken us, but once we are awake, the true adventure is ready to begin.

CHAPTER 9

Spiritual Science

spiritual science

Mr. Ludy," Purity began, "I have only two things to say."

"OK," I agreed. "I'm listening."

"I've been in this business a long time, my friend. And what I am about to tell you has been proven in the laboratory of life millions upon millions of times over. You could call it spiritual science."

I enthusiastically prepared myself to begin writing.

"The first thing I wish to say is this." Purity sat back in his seat and fiddled with a little carton of dairy creamer. "Until one learns to admire me, value my ways, appreciate my manner, and fully embrace my role in the process, one will never meet Great Sex."

I opened my mouth to ask a question, but Mr. Purity continued his passionate explanation. "You see, Mr. Ludy, the habit one develops in relating to me is the habit one will adopt for handling everything that follows me. God cannot and will not give that which is precious, valuable, and eternal to those who treat it as if it were ordinary and mundane. He reserves His finest jewels for those who prove aficionados of His finery."

Everything was starting to make sense to me now. "Is that why you wouldn't let me interview you until I had passed your tests?"

"That's precisely why," Purity stated. "I am the gatekeeper for the whole kit and caboodle of everything precious in Christ's kingdom. If you treat me with contempt, then I'll prohibit you from going any further. Believe me, I'm not turning over Sacred to someone who won't treat her with great respect, nor will I let some self-centered, thrill-seeking rabble come near Great Sex."

"So . . ." I attempted to sneak in a question, but Mr. Purity was on a roll.

"You came prancing along with this idea for a book about Great Sex, and I nearly had a heart attack. Here you were, planning to take some very sacred things and make them public. I thought the Almighty was going to clamp down on this project and mortify you with a deep conviction, and I was certain you would never get near Great Sex for an interview. But Mr. Ludy, you did something that changed everything. You honored me. You respected my position. You allowed me to do things in your heart and life, very painful things I'm rarely invited to do in any soul. Mr. Ludy, you appreciate my ways, my manner. You admire who I am, and you fully appraise my strength and importance. Therefore, even though this is a sacred procedure, you have been ushered forward down the most holy, ancient corridors."

"Does this mean," I blurted excitedly, "that I'm finally going to be able to interview Great Sex?"

"No, it does not!" Purity said strongly, causing our entire table to tremble. "We are in unprecedented territory here, Mr. Ludy. Introducing Great Sex in a published book is like strolling into the holy of holies with a film crew—it's just not done."

I took a sip from my now-cooled chai tea and wished my latest question could be deleted from the transcript. I was in definite need of a bit more patience in this process.

"The second thing I wish to say is this." Purity adjusted his mammoth body in the small chair and continued. "The journey toward Great Sex is intended to be fun." With that, a smile spread across his face. "It seems most people who throw my name around in Christian circles today have a perpetually dour expression. You would think I was a funeral dirge or a kidney stone! But contrary to popular belief, I'm the opening act for the greatest action drama of anyone's life. I set the stage for heavenly love stories that leave Hollywood's lusty counterfeits blushing with bewilderment."

He tossed the small dairy creamer carton into the air and caught it in his meaty hand. "What I am about to say, Mr. Ludy, I realize that you personally may already know, but I want you to write it down anyway."

I looked up at him with pen poised for action, proving my eagerness to comply.

"Great Sex is never found by those who misconstrue me for Jack the Ripper. Frowns and complaints don't win anyone a backstage pass to meet the cast of this great love story. The only thing frowns and complaints will get you is my disregard. I can't stand a complainer. I'm here for one purpose—to make people's lives beautiful and amazing—so when the complaints start flowing, I stop working. It's that simple. If people want the best, they need to be prepared for a little pain, a little discomfort, and a little hard work. Olympians are not forged in front of televisions sitting on comfy couches; they're made in the fires of physical training. Great lovers are made the very same way, my friend."

I nodded my approval as I wrote down his observations. "This is good stuff!"

"It's spiritual science, Mr. Ludy . . . spiritual science." With that, Mr. Purity sat back in his chair and took a gulp from his large mug of black coffee, indicating that our interview was over.

I looked over my notes and reflected on our conversation. What Mr. Purity said was truly profound, but the way he shared it made it seem so obvious and elementary. In essence he was saying, be hospitable to Purity and Purity will be hospitable to you. And seeing as how Purity is the gatekeeper for everything precious and blissful in God's kingdom, currying Purity's favor isn't a bad idea.

And I liked how he said that Purity is all about a greater pleasure and fulfillment. Purity's about fun. And even though his work might sting, it's only temporary, and it is necessary to unlock the extraordinary joy that follows. So we shouldn't complain when Purity is busy working in our souls; rather, we should get excited—for the stage is being set for something amazing to follow.

Mr. Purity is right. I deeply admire who Purity is and appreciate how Purity works. Everything he said, I've personally seen proven in the laboratory of my own life. But what I've realized through writing this book and encountering Mr. Purity in this new way is that he is a lot bigger, a lot stronger, and a lot more magnificent, and even more fun, than I had ever known.

When you first relinquish the controls of your life to Jesus Christ, expect to meet this gigantic hulking dude. But don't shy away from the conviction he will certainly bring. He's only setting the stage for a better, bigger, fuller, more satisfying existence.

CHAPTER 10

Sacred Interview

In the previous chapter, I may have misled you into believing that when Mr. Purity stopped talking, he finished his cup of coffee, shook my hand, and walked out. But what actually happened is much more interesting.

Mr. Purity said, "It's spiritual science, Mr. Ludy . . . spiritual science." And then, as if those words were a cue, the front door of the café jangled and in strolled his breathtaking love interest.

Mr. Purity had his back toward the door, but he seemed to instinctively know that Sacred was near.

"Hello, dear," he said warmly, standing to his feet in honor of our new guest.

"Hello, doll," she replied as she stood on her toes and tenderly kissed his cheek.

I quickly jumped up and grabbed a chair for Sacred, making sure she wasn't disappointed this go-around with my gentlemanly manners.

"Hello, Peeps," she greeted politely.

"Ma'am," I stuttered, feeling oafish and awkward, not quite knowing what to say or do with someone of such heavenly refinement.

She giggled.

"Did I do something wrong?" I asked, turning a deep shade of red.

"No, no." she smiled. "It's just so nice to see a man even try. And Mr. Ludy, it's not precisely *what* you do, but it's that you are *willing* to do it that really matters to a lady. You are a gentleman already in your marriage with Leslie, and you highly esteem that which is Sacred, but I would be remiss if I didn't tell you that I still have much to teach you." She smiled warmly.

"I know, I know," I grimaced. "I'm still a beginner."

"Precisely," said Sacred. "But being a beginner is not all bad. It means you still have great discoveries and great achievements awaiting you."

The three of us sat down.

"Peeps," Sacred asked, "do you know why Mr. Purity and I have been elusive, mysterious, and understated throughout this process?"

"Well, you said it was to make the process more fun."

"Yes, but more fun for whom?"

"I guess I've been thinking more fun for all of you." I paused and thought it through for a second. "But the fact that you are asking that question leads me to consider the idea that you are being elusive and mysterious in order to make this process more fun for *me*."

"Another astute observation," she exclaimed with a wide grin. "You are a very good student."

I pondered this concept for a few seconds. As I considered what my next question should be, Sacred spoke.

"You have a deadline for your book, do you not?"

"Yes."

"Life is full of deadlines, dear friend, full of reasons to rush things, skip along the surface of life rather than dig down into the true meat of it."

"That's definitely true."

"Well, the reason God assigned me to be a part of your spiritual development is to bring enjoyment, colorful dimension, and romance into your life."

I nodded, interested and very willing to never have a book deadline hanging over my head again.

"My job," Sacred continued, "is to teach you to appreciate sacred things, to place value on the things of God's kingdom, to slow you down in order that you might smell the roses He is planting inside your life."

"I always thought that Holiness was the formation of Christ's life within my own, in order to make my life showcase His divine nature."

"Very good, Peeps. That is precisely what I do. But I don't facilitate that heavenly process for fake grins and half-hearted giggles. I do it so that your soul can smile so big it hurts. I do it so you can love wildly with passion and purpose. I do it so you can fully comprehend the stunning value of the Cross. I do it so that you will never take lightly the gift of God's very life living, moving, and having His being within your body."

She paused to bring emphasis to her upcoming statement. "I do what I do, dearest Peeps, to make your face shine, your heart pound, your feet dance, and your lips sing with delight. I'm the one assigned by the Holy Spirit to remind a soul how truly good the gospel is, how truly magnificent our God is, and how truly breathtaking His plans are for you."

Those hundred puppy dogs were yelping and hopping about within her eyes. She was radiant, enraptured as she spoke. It was as if she lived in the presence of God and was now attempting to describe to me what it is all really like.

"Peeps, when you realize that you have something precious, you will protect it. So it's my job to show you how precious what you have in Christ really is."

"This is good stuff," I said, scribbling down everything she was saying and realizing that I was desperately lacking creativity in my choice of exclamations.

"While Mr. Purity is building the stage," she continued, "I'm the one in charge of set design. God is the producer of the drama, and I'm the one He's chosen to be the choreographer. I do what I do with the intent of sparking interest, piquing fascination, and wooing the crowd to beg for more and more of Christ."

"So how does this relate to Great Sex?" I asked a bit sheepishly.

"Learn to be great with Jesus Christ, dear friend, and you will, by natural course, be great with Sex."

"So," I said, "if Mr. Purity is the protective force behind the League, would it be accurate to call you the romantic force?"

She paused before answering, biting her bottom lip as she considered the idea. "Holiness is the essence of romance, dear one—the very essence!" Her enthusiasm grew as she continued, "I give the human heart wings in order to soar with the ecstasy of adoration and longing. When I am allowed to cull a soul, I train it to fully appreciate its object of affection, whether that be

Jesus Christ or even an earthly lover. I equip it to fully enjoy that great love with all the arts of intimacy at heaven's disposal."

She glanced over at Mr. Purity and he prompted her to continue.

"You see, Peeps, all I care about is the fame and renown of Jesus Christ. And when my name falls into the mud, it is impossible for God's people to rightly comprehend and relate to their true King, let alone applaud His majesty. It is I who make a human soul ready for a divine relationship with Christ, and subsequently, I make a human heart ready for a supernaturally charged romance with a spouse. When the idea of Holiness is lost, then something far worse than Great Sex falls into obscurity—a truly victorious and utterly triumphant engagement with the God of the universe is also lost."

As I jotted down these truths, I asked, "Why is Holiness such a pivotal point in a God encounter?"

"Without it souls are merely slogging along out of human effort, human duty, and human mentalities. I am the catalyst for the life, love, and power of Almighty God overtaking the human existence so that it is no longer them living, controlling, and defining their existences but God in them, operating the controls and making a name for Himself."

Sacred leaned forward with intensity. "Mr. Ludy, Jesus Christ is after the most pure and perfect love relationship with His Bride, and I am the one who lights the fire of adoration, stokes the flame of divine love, and blows upon the embers of intimacy. I train a soul in the mystery, the mystique, the magic of sacred words, sacred moments, sacred songs, and sacred touches. I teach a soul to wait even when it is urged by the flesh to move forward quickly. I teach a heart to guard its emotions so that the emotions are pure when finally released. I teach a soul how to discern the sacred God-orchestrated moments for progression. In short, Mr. Ludy, I make this whole drama with Christ and with an earthly lover a bit of heaven on earth."

I couldn't help but admire her as she spoke. She was glowing. I was witnessing her deepest passion, her deepest purpose, and it was an astounding sort of beauty to behold. Sacred was impossible not to adore. She seemed to effervesce the sweetest perfume of Christ and usher me headlong into the holy of holies. When I listened to her, I wanted everything she offered. And I guess the thing that shocked me most of all is that everything she wished to bring to my life was already mine, purchased by Jesus Christ Himself two thousand years ago.

There was a long silence at our table. Purity and Sacred must have known I couldn't handle any more at the moment, for they sat silently with me as I tried to assimilate this gargantuan truth. I was literally overcome with amazement. In the past half hour or so, I had literally had an encounter with Jesus Christ. In listening to Purity and Sacred gush their deepest purpose, I found myself tapping into *my* deepest purpose—more and more of Him.

As much as I didn't want to admit it yet, I was realizing that this book about Great Sex was actually becoming something much bigger—a book about a Great God!

And I was also beginning to realize that this circuitous writing process was rather fun. It was suspenseful, full of surprise and speckled with sacred moments along the way. Purity and Holiness were actually making the journey toward an interview with Great Sex really fun, really beautiful, and . . . get this . . . *really romantic!* Everything I had experienced prior in my love story with Leslie was being replayed in my journey to write this book. And the parallels were uncanny. As much as I didn't know how the story would turn out back then, I didn't know how it was all going to turn out now.

☐ ☐ ☐

My conversations with Mr. Purity and Sacred ended on a pleasant, albeit mysterious note. As we were preparing to leave, I asked, "So when should I expect the next interview?"

Mr. Purity and Sacred looked at me and grinned.

"Let's just say," Sacred remarked coyly, "it will be after another test."

"Another test?" I squirmed.

"Don't worry, dear one," Sacred soothed, "this one won't be quite as painful. In fact, you might find this one to be quite fun."

With a twinkle in her eye and a parting smile, she grabbed hold of Mr. Purity's arm and exited with him through the jangling door. I decided to come home to my lovely wife and debrief, in hopes of spending the rest of the day processing what had transpired that morning.

So here I am now, sitting at my laptop, attempting to make sense of this interview material. With thoughts of "Mr. Ludy, you're merely a beginner at this whole Sex thing" skipping about inside my head, I have seriously questioned my ability to continue even writing this book. After all, I was not intending this book to be the inexperienced ramblings of a beginner. I thought I was an expert. I thought what Leslie and I shared in our marriage was pure and utter bliss. I thought we had this whole Great Sex thing figured out.

When I arrived back from Loodles, I dumped all of this raw emotion on Leslie and she unflinchingly stated back to me, "Beef, just because we only know Sex at a beginner's level doesn't mean what we share in our marriage is *not* pure and utter bliss. It doesn't mean we haven't found the lost treasure. And it certainly doesn't mean we haven't figured some things out!"

"But . . ." I protested.

"But what?" she responded. "I think it is amazing to realize that what we have is only the beginner's version. Just think what we can discover tomorrow, and the next day, and the next day after that!"

She had a point. In fact, the more I thought about Leslie's remarks, the more I realized that maybe I *was* a good person to be writing this book. After all, I know the artistry of Great Sex personally, so I can speak with courage, confidence, and credibility regarding his existence. But I also am still only a beginner in my understanding and experience, so that lends me that much-needed authentic, down-to-earth, I-am-in-this-whole-mess-with-you dimension that modern readers seem to appreciate.

So, in summary, I've decided to keep pressing forward in this adventure. And I'm not going to make any excuses along the way for the fact that I'm learning right along with you. If you are in agreement with that, then I say let's move this whole thing forward.

◻ ◻ ◻

Why do I need yet another test? I've been asking myself that question over and over again. But I'm starting to unfold a mystery here. God doesn't just want me to have head knowledge *about* truth; He wants me to intimately share in the power of truth at work in my life.

Mr. Purity could have just spoken truth, but instead he used a test to press truth into the deepest corners of my soul. Then when he spoke, I had an entirely new level of understanding.

If Sacred were merely to talk about the grandeur of the kingdom of God and about the beauty of Jesus Christ but never actually introduce me to that glorious reality at the depths of my soul, then what good would she really have done for me? It is the test that drives the truth deep into the muscle of the soul. It is the test that allows truths to become living realities, good ideas to become beautiful certainties, and profound thoughts to become working actualities.

Are tests fun? Not if you don't realize what they are for. But when you begin to comprehend that tests are a critical part of the journey toward, not just Great Sex, but the fuller understanding of Jesus Christ—they actually become fun!

I'm looking forward to this test. Of course, I have a bit of trepidation about it, but I really am excited. What Mr. Purity has taken me through these past four weeks was difficult, but it was also liberating and life giving. Whatever Sacred has up her sleeve, I trust that it will only draw me closer to Jesus Christ and ever closer to an even greater rendition of Sex.

I started this book thinking that since I've experienced the blessings of Great Sex firsthand I could go book him for a public interview. But I've discovered that there is a pattern for accessing Great Sex. It is the same pattern for a single person approaching marriage as it is for a married couple approaching their fiftieth wedding anniversary. And ironically, it is the same pattern, whether the encounter with Sex is for private enjoyment or, as in this case, for public education. All I can say is—it was fun to explore this pattern when I was single and I was experiencing this adventure for the very first time, but, as strange as this might sound . . . *it is even more fun now.*

CHAPTER 11

Becoming a Kook

C ould I talk with you?" Deuce Johnson whispered to me conspiratorially while standing on the other side of the cash register. "In private?"

Seven days had slipped by since Deuce had even looked at me, let alone spoken to me. The clumsy thrusting of my manuscript upon his unsuspecting soul, as detailed in chapter 8, for some reason hadn't produced the result I had expected. I had pictured him smiling big, giving me a huge hug, and saying, "Thank you, Eric! I really needed to hear that!" Instead, I received a cold shoulder. And whereas Deuce typically was a congenial, albeit crude, sort of fellow, this past week he had been stomping about as if he had lost a crucial lug nut to his sanity, and his cold shoulder was especially frigid.

So I think you will understand that when he asked me if we could talk in private, I swallowed hard and struggled to answer. "Ah . . . sure thing," I stammered.

"Could we do it now?" he asked with intensity.

"OK, yeah," I agreed. "Definitely."

Ever since my interview with Purity and Sacred a week ago, I had been sitting around waiting for Sacred's "test." To my chagrin, I had become dependent upon the League in providing the information I needed about Great Sex. Authors typically like to depend on their own ingenuity and their own individual flair for eloquence when writing, but minus the input of my new friends from the League, I was stuck under a five-hundred-pound case of good old-fashioned writer's block.

Sacred's parting words to me seven days previous had been about some kind of a test. I was actually welcoming this test because at least it could possibly scare up some good content for this book. But here I was a week later, and nothing even resembling a test seemed to be transpiring in my life. At night I dreamed of unmet book deadlines, and during the day I sat and stared at my computer screen hoping my fingers would just happen to type something intelligent.

"Leslie," I said to my wife on the morning of the seventh day, "would you mind if I head over to Loodles to try to get some writing in today?"

"Are you sure you shouldn't wait until you hear from the League again?"

"It's been seven days!" I barked, letting off a little steam. "This manuscript is due in less than two months, and I'm still nowhere close to getting an interview with Great Sex!"

"Well, maybe that's the test," she reasoned. "Maybe Sacred wants to be the one governing the writing of this book."

To say that I disregarded Leslie's statement is too strong a description. I would never disregard my wife's reasoning.

I just often don't fully appraise its brilliance when it first arrives.

On day seven, Leslie figured out the test and, let's just say, it took me a little while longer to figure out what my wife already knew. Sacred was waiting for the reins. She was ready to teach me some of the most profound spiritual truths I had ever encountered—but first, I had to let go of the controls of this book.

Instead of saying, "Leslie, you're brilliant!" I launched into a seventeen-and-a-half-minute tirade on the ethics of upholding contracts and turning in manuscripts on time until my lovely bride was coerced into saying, "Beef, my day would be a lot sweeter if you packed up your computer and went to Loodles!"

So there I was at Loodles, preparing to talk with Deuce Johnson. This wasn't exactly what I expected when I headed out that morning, but I had been learning in this process to embrace the bizarre as it comes.

I found a small table over by the window, grabbed a coaster, and positioned my hot chai along the far edge of the table, and then set up my laptop.

In a couple of minutes, Deuce arrived at the table with his latte—and a couple of churlish dudes at his side.

"Would you mind," Deuce asked, "if I grab a couple more chairs for my friends?"

"Not at all," I mumbled, wondering what else I could say in such a situation. *I thought he wanted to talk in private!*

The two men looked familiar, though I couldn't quite place them. "Do you guys work out at the Miramont club?" I asked politely, attempting to generate a little looseness in the atmosphere.

"No," barked the heavyset one, who nearly knocked me out with his tobacco breath as he sat down on a chair beside me.

"Are you from Windsor?"

The two of them looked at me as if I were speaking a foreign language and grunted their disapproval of my chosen spot near the window.

"Deuce," the tobacco-breathing, plump guy growled, "would you mind asking your friend here to adios his laptop and give the rest of us some space?"

I took the hint. I folded up my laptop and stuck it in my briefcase on the floor.

"Mr. Ludy, I'm going to get right to the point." It was the second of the two men who spoke—the thin one. He would have been a handsome chap except for his irritating, smarmy grin. "We don't particularly care for your brand of religion."

I was taken aback by his remark. I looked at the man, trying hard to remember where I had seen him before. He looked a bit like a washed-up Las Vegas magician, with a bizarre mustache as well as the corniest pair of black-rimmed glasses I'd ever seen. I wanted to say something in response, but I had no idea what would sound even the least bit intelligent.

"It's puritanical, Bible-thumping, holier-than-thou bigots like you," snorted the fat one, "who make Christianity so dog-gone uptight and prudish."

"Excuse me," I said, interjecting myself into the man's tirade, "but who are you guys?"

"Let's just say we're advocates for human rights," coughed the meaty-cheeked one. "I can sniff out bigots like you from a mile away. You're all the same, and the pollution you jam into people's minds is criminal."

I looked over at Deuce. "I thought you wanted to meet with me in private."

"I did," Deuce said with a shrug, "but these guys forced themselves in."

"Do you know them?"

"Yeah," he grimaced apologetically.

"Listen to me, Mr. Ludy," the smarmy one grunted. "We're seriously considering filing harassment charges over this whole forced-read manuscript debacle."

"Harassment charges?" Again I looked at Deuce. "Is there a hidden camera around here somewhere? Are these guys actually serious?"

"We're dead serious," insisted the big one.

"And from what Mr. Johnson here says," said the thin one, "we also may be able to pin you for slander and libel."

"Who did I slander?"

"According to Mr. Johnson, there was a deliberate act of malfeasance on your part on page 33 of your manuscript, falsely accusing our client of speaking ill about a victim of special needs. If you publish that trash, we'll see you in court!"

I shook my head in disbelief and stood up from my seat.

"Don't go, Eric," Deuce pleaded.

"Don't go?" I said with disbelief, "You are accusing me of harassment, slander, and libel, Deuce. And you and I both know that there isn't a shred of truth in any of those accusations."

"I know," Deuce responded sheepishly.

The two churlish men turned to face Deuce. "We have recorded testimony from you, Mr. Johnson, stating otherwise!" croaked the fat one with a snort.

"Deuce!" the other one stammered, "if you go soft on us, it's over! It's all over! We've gone over this and over this, and I've warned you that if you give up our representation, you give up all our perks too!"

I had picked up my bag to leave, but I paused to consider what was happening here.

"Help me!" said Deuce, barely above a whisper.

"He can't help you!" growled the plump guy, slamming his fist on the small table. "This Ludy guy's a kook! He wants you to believe you can live without our aid. That's impossible. We've made you who you are! We are the reason you are so popular. This guy will shred your reputation and stick your name in the gutter right next to his!"

Suddenly I was fully aware of who it was that was sharing a table with me and Deuce. It was none other than Jimmy the Shrimp in all his plump splendor, and, if you removed the black-rimmed glasses and the hideous mustache off his tall, funny-shaped sidekick, he was none other than Imposter Sex. This conversation wasn't about me; it was about Deuce. Deuce was a soul in the stew and he must be starting to lean toward Jesus. These guys were scared.

"Deuce," I spoke softly but forcefully, "you don't need these guys. And if you turn to Jesus Christ, these two fiends no longer will have you under their thumbs. They no longer will have control."

"But I don't want what you have!" Deuce protested.

"What do I have that you don't want?" I asked, curious.

"I guess it's more what you don't have," Deuce muttered.

"You mean," I said, "I don't have casual, meaningless sex? I don't masturbate, and I don't need pornography to satisfy my inner life? Is that what you are afraid to give up?"

"Hey now!" spat the fat one. "Why don't you take your tasteless religion and give it to someone who can stomach its insanity!"

"Don't listen to him, Mr. Johnson!" urged the thin one. "This Ludy guy is a kook! He's a Christian, and you know Christians are mentally unstable!"

"Deuce," I interjected, "what you read last week in my manuscript is true. And if you are interested, I can introduce you to the One who can make it a vibrant reality in your life."

"I don't want to be a religious kook like you," Deuce insisted. "I know you mean well, and you're a good tipper, but you're also a purity freak."

"But you saw Mr. Purity with your own eyes, Deuce," I reminded him. "You saw who he really is. You saw him correctly! And you know good and well that he isn't some feeble-minded weakling."

"Yeah, but I know how everyone else will see him."

Right there was the classic argument of Jimmy the Shrimp's regime. The cigar-smoking Mob boss had been using that line of reasoning since time immemorial to stop the forward progress of a soul in the stew. The reasoning went something like this: "Sure I might see him correctly, but no one else will see him that way—everyone else will see him as a spineless nerf and think I'm a bonehead for following such an idiotic path." This was the ultimate appeal to self. It screamed, "Consider self above God. Consider reputation above truth. Consider temporal worldly applause above all eternal matters. Eat a bowl full of red stew now and pass on the inheritance of heaven later." This was classic Shrimp!

"Come on, Deuce. You have to think about what's best for

you," said the heavyset one, oozing with feigned compassion. "You've got a lot to lose. And it's not just your reputation. It's all your girls, your pleasures, your wild fun, and even your future as a rock guitarist might be in jeopardy here!"

"Deuce," I interjected, "the God of the universe has placed His finger on your soul. He's asking for your life. And He's asking you to trust Him, no matter the cost."

"Why give everything up for a load of fables?" barked the big one.

"Christians know nothing about Sex," breathed the thin one venomously.

"And even if this whole Christianity thing were true," continued the Shrimp, "the price is far too high for what you get in return."

"They make Sex off limits," Imposter Sex propounded, "but if you stick with us, you can get it any time you want it, and we will never make you feel guilty!"

"Why would you ever even think," crooned Jimmy the Shrimp, "of wanting to be like this kook Ludy?"

"The guy's got nothing on you!" shouted Imposter Sex.

"You're wrong!" answered Deuce. "Eric is on to something. I can see it! And what he's writing about is something too!"

"But you don't need it!" cried Jimmy the Shrimp.

"I'm dying without it," whimpered Deuce, desperately trying to work his way through the fog. "And I want what he has, even if I have to look like a kook to get it!"

"Nothing is worth that much!" said Imposter Sex.

"Jesus is worth it, Deuce," I assured him, "and a million times more!"

Deuce turned and looked at me, tears in his eyes and a look

of anguish on his face. "I want whatever you have, Eric, and I'm willing to give up whatever is necessary to get it!" Then he paused and added, "At least I think I am."

This conversation went on for another ten minutes. The voices of Jimmy the Shrimp and Imposter Sex echoed on and on about the risks, the dangers, and the stupidity of such a decision. Witnessing the battle of a soul in the stew is something that makes your stomach churn. I remember being right where Deuce was, longing for something more but surrounded by the churlish voices that sounded so wise and so committed to my best interests. When I realized that my words weren't accomplishing anything, I closed my eyes and bowed my head to pray for Deuce.

"What are you doing?" Deuce asked.

I didn't answer him. Instead, I silently prayed for his soul. I prayed that God would enable Deuce to cry out for his assistance in this battle. I prayed that Deuce would turn to Jesus Christ for rescue.

A full minute passed before Deuce asked me again, "What are you doing? Are you praying?" Then he said something that sent chills up my spine. Through the cacophony of all the false counsel he urged, "Pray for me, Eric, please!"

I continued to pray. And the strangest thing happened. It was as if the volume of the fat man and the thin man's voices were actually turned down and the volume of God's Spirit speaking within the soul of Deuce Johnson was suddenly turned up.

"Could you ask Jesus a question for me, Eric?" Deuce begged.

I opened my eyes and said, "You can ask Him for yourself if you would like."

"I don't feel comfortable with that. He doesn't know me at all."

"Oh, He knows you, Deuce. He knows you better than you know yourself. And He's been aching to have you ask Him a question for a long, long time."

Deuce looked down at his hands awkwardly, then he blurted out, "Jesus, help me!"

The next hour was quite supernatural and full of grace. The moment Deuce implored the help of Jesus, his counselors stood up and headed for the door. I can't tell you how pleasant it was, sitting at that small table for those next sixty minutes, to talk with Deuce in peace without cigar breath and heavy cologne polluting the air. Deuce Johnson, one of the most unlikely characters to ever sing in a church choir, was transformed. No longer was he a soul in the stew, but rather a soul basking in the perfect peace and joy of heaven's love.

Near the end of our time together, he asked me a significant question. It went something like this: "Will I ever have to deal with Jimmy the Shrimp and Imposter Sex again, or am I officially through with them?"

"That is a very good question," I responded. This may be a question that you probably have asked in the past, are asking now, or will ask when you yourself go through your own personalized Deuce-like spiritual makeover. So I'll tell you what I told Deuce.

"If you don't want to ever listen to their voices again, then I'm happy to tell you . . . *you never have to.* But you must realize that Jimmy the Shrimp and all his evil cohorts will never stop talking. Twenty-four hours a day they talk, trying to convince you to stop your spiritual progress and pleading for you to think about yourself again—but you can turn down the volume of their voices by turning your attention to Christ's voice. I can tell you from personal experience that there may be times when you find yourself once again listening to that cigar-smoking cheese head, but when you do, don't run from God in shame—instead, run to God immediately, ask forgiveness, and begin listening to His holy, loving voice afresh from that moment forward."

Dear reader, I recognize that this is a strange sort of a book. It is supposedly about Great Sex, but it hardly has even mentioned that grand subject. I realize that you may find little fascination in a young man named Deuce Johnson. However, it is important to note that Deuce Johnson is more than just a barista working in Cup of Loodles Café, in Windsor, Colorado. He is also symbolic of something.

Deuce is you and me.

He is you and me—struggling to listen to Christ's voice over Jimmy the Shrimp's bellowing.

He is you and me—yearning to believe that Mr. Purity won't ruin our lives and that Sacred won't utterly destroy us.

He is you and me—risking everything in hopes of finding something better than the cheap imitation version of love, romance, and sex this world offers us on a plastic hospital tray while we lie prostrate in critical spiritual condition wheezing with despair.

There is a bit of Deuce Johnson in each of us.

The question is which way is the Deuce within us going to turn, and which voice is he going to heed? The way you answer that question will define the failure or success of your entire life.

CHAPTER 12

Sacred Waiting

I haven't written anything in this book for the last forty-nine days. And whereas, the book-writing, deadline-toting, need-to-get-something-done-today-or-I'm-a-good-for-nothing-louse part of me struggled a bit throughout these past seven weeks, there was another part of me that came to life in an entirely new way.

This morning represented the forty-second morning since Deuce Johnson's transformation, but it is the forty-*ninth* morning since Sacred promised me that there would be another test. I admit that the first week of this "test," I was a bit cantankerous and not quite ready to accept what Sacred needed to do in my life. But the Deuce Johnson encounter (chronicled in chapter 11) shook me up a bit and got me thinking about what I have in Christ and what I'd be willing to give up to keep it.

You see, Sacred, just like when I first met her prior to my love story with Leslie, was asking to hold in her keeping the things that should belong to God and yet were still under my control. In my past, they were my sexual desires, my thoughts, my future, my right to be married, my career, my ability to choose—the list goes on and on. Basically, everything in my life that now is considered God's property started out in *my* possession. So the longer that list is, the better, as far as Sacred is concerned.

Sacred has asked me to give up many things over the years, but this time around, she was asking for something rather odd. And, to be honest, it was something that seemed rather strange to give up. She wanted *this book*.

Leslie and I pride ourselves in turning in writing projects on time. But Sacred was saying, "Your writing is sacred work, Peeps, so I need it in my keeping!"

These past forty-nine days have been something special. No. Let me correct that. Something *very* special. As I followed Sacred's lead, she led me into a land flowing with milk and honey.

I picked up a small blue note from my pillowcase just this morning. It read:

Peeps! I'm bursting with excitement to hear what you thought about my latest test! Loodles, 10:00 a.m.

I had a grand smile on my face as I read the simple note. After wiping the sleep from my eyes and unleashing a very large yawn, I leaned over and kissed Leslie and chuckled to myself about Sacred's latest masterpiece.

"What's so funny?" Leslie asked.

"Oh, nothing. I was just thinking about how good God is, that's all."

"He is good, isn't He?" Leslie smiled big to match my toothy grin.

"I love you soooooo much," I crooned, kissing her one more time for good measure.

"You sure are frisky for five o'clock in the morning," Leslie laughed.

"Get ready for a lot more frisky!" I hollered, hopping out of bed. "This guy," I said, craning my thumb back against my chest, "is officially going to be moving past the beginner's level!"

"Oh, really?" Leslie waggled her eyebrows at me.

"That's right!" I thundered, draping a bathrobe around me and moseying toward the bathroom. "No more Mr. Mediocre! I've got some friends who are teaching me a thing or two!"

"You got a note from the League, didn't you?" she observed with a wry grin.

"Yep!" I said, as I strolled in front of the bathroom sink. "So move over Mr. Mediocre, and say hello to Mr. Marvelous!"

OK, I realize that this may be a bit too heavy on the mush for all of you faint of heart, but you must realize that, sappy or not, when Sacred does her work, sparks start flying, sweet words are spoken, love songs are sung with newfound ardor, and big and glorious dreams for the future are hatched. Becoming, *ahem*, Mr. Marvelous just happens to be one of *my* dreams.

It took me an unfortunate chunk of time to actually figure out what Sacred's "test" was. And yes, Leslie had the riddle solved after only seven days, but as a man, I pride myself in taking much longer to deduce things in the arena of love and sex.

So even though I got a rather late start, I spent the past forty-nine days of "testing" loving and cherishing my wife in new and beautiful ways. I have been writing an inordinate amount of love letters to her, kissing her more times per day than ever in our marriage, pondering her beauty throughout the day, and whispering love sonnets to her when I'm supposed to be writing this book. I have spent more time cuddling with Leslie in these past seven weeks than is probably legal for any author to spend and still consider himself a valid author. I'm thinking that possibly my occupation title should officially switch from author to lover. And this, my friends, is the work of Sacred.

Is the work of Sacred something to fear? Is it something I should have shied away from? Is having Holiness overtake and overshadow my existence going to make me a bland, dull, colorless creature waddling about all day, chewing cud, and grazing woefully in the dry flowerless grasses of God's kingdom?

That's simply ridiculous!

The more that Purity and Holiness overtake my life, the more I find myself singing, experiencing pure and utter joy, and wanting to share what I have with everyone I meet. It shouldn't surprise me, because that's exactly what Leslie and I found so many years ago during the formation of our love story.

When Leslie and I surrendered the pen of our life to the Author of romance, He ushered Purity and Holiness into our midst. The decisions we made as a result of Sacred's counsel wouldn't have seemed very appealing to those who had never met her. From the outside looking in, most would have assumed that she was causing us to miss out on all the fun of being young and in love. After all, we didn't say "I love you" until the night of our engagement, we refrained from almost all physical expressions of affection, and we didn't even kiss until our wedding day. Most would see that as an extreme, unnecessary, and rather depressing way to nurture a blossoming romance. Most would assume that as a result of those decisions, we ended up with a solemn-faced, second-rate version of love.

But to any who make that assumption, all I can say is—*you weren't there!* Leslie and I didn't make those choices because of duty or obligation. We made those decisions in order to honor the sacred things in our love story, things most people treat with carelessness and disregard. We wanted to restore the luster and polish to romance by reserving each and every forward step for the God-scripted moment.

And what we found as a result was nothing short of a fairy tale.

In a generation where love stories have been reduced to blasé, haphazard relationships that lose their sparkle as quickly as a Fourth of July fireworks display, Leslie and I have found something amazing. Something lifelong. Something worth writing eleven books (and counting) about. All because of Purity and Holiness.

I honestly want every last one of you reading this book to discover, in your own marriages, what I share in my marriage with Leslie. It is pure and holy yet perfectly romantic and delectably fun! I'm a guy who likes to smile and laugh, and Purity and Holiness are the great instigators of the belly laugh that leaves you a helpless pile on the floor, the radiant smile you just can't seem to remove from your face, and the jubilant song that just has to be sung at the very top of your lungs.

Many of us miss out on the blessing of Sacred's tests because the tests she metes out don't come in the package we want or expect. At the behest of God, Sacred asks for us to relinquish control of things that we deem "ours." Sacred wants to take our lives and choreograph the most amazing drama, the most entertaining Broadway musical, and the most satisfying action-adventure.

But to do that, she needs everything that is currently under our control to be transferred into her "sacred keeping." If our life is to be beautiful, it is because Sacred is setting the stage, conducting the instruments, and orchestrating the mood of life's grand story. Sacred is the only one who can show us how we can take this life of ours and effectively love another life with it. She's the only one who can direct us *how* and *when* to share the most sacred aspects of our existence with our spouse.

Sacred is the foremost expert in the universe at the art of romance and the perfectly timed expressions of adoration and love. She is the grand set designer for Great Sex, and she is a master at drawing out the majesty of a single glorious moment so that it is never to be forgotten. And as I have discovered over these past forty-nine days, she is also the one who must hold and direct the pen when a book is being written.

When Sacred is working her magic and choreographing our lives, she has one principal tool that she uses time and time again. She loves to make us *wait*. Now, I realize that sounds abhorrent and wholly unromantic, but it is actually quite the contrary.

We live in a fast-food, microwavable, Internet-download-able society and the idea of waiting for *anything* is tantamount to returning to cooking over an open fire and pacing in front of dial-up modems. But waiting is the chief ingredient in every great romantic tale. For it is through cherishing the "waiting" seasons of life that we learn to fully appreciate and take delight in the "receiving" seasons.

There is a sacred and appointed time for everything in God's kingdom. It is the time in which everything God made can be fully appreciated and fully enjoyed. Whether that is a lunar eclipse, a bud of lilac during the spring, the day we whisper "I do" to our dear lover, or even the return of our majestic King Jesus to claim His own—everything appreciated is something that was first *anticipated*. Sacred is in the business of building anticipation, and therefore, appreciation.

During these past seven weeks Sacred has been reminding me how enchanted my life really is, building my appreciation through anticipation. In other words, I've been doing a lot of "sacred waiting." Sacred waiting isn't twiddling thumbs, but rather prayerful anticipation and expectation of God.

"Les?" I said sweetly to my wife as I was preparing to leave the house this morning for Loodles. "Doesn't this feel just like our love story?"

"It's better!" she said, kissing my cheek.

It is true that I'm no longer waiting for my future spouse or waiting to discover Great Sex for the first time, but at every season of our life Sacred finds the ideal things for which we can learn to wait all over again. And when we embrace these seasons of "sacred waiting," it is amazing how much our relationship with Jesus Christ is amplified and every other relationship in our lives has the opportunity to flourish.

To reach Great Sex, both Mr. Purity and Sacred had to work on me. But Mr. Purity and Sacred work in completely different ways. Mr. Purity cleans our house, while Sacred furnishes our house and makes it smell like apple pie and freshly picked daffodils. Mr. Purity brings conviction and uproots all the junk taking up space within our souls so that nothing can hinder the Life of Christ within. Sacred, however, grooms and shapes our lives so that we can fully enjoy the Life of Christ within. Mr. Purity's favorite tool is conviction, while Sacred's favorite tool is waiting.

In the forty-nine-day waiting period that Sacred arranged for me during the writing of this book, Sacred lined up for us three very specific sacred waiting opportunities.

Sacred Waiting Opportunity #1: Waiting for a Child. Leslie and I have been waiting for quite some time for another child—a little brother or sister for Hudson. And we are nearly bursting at the seams with excitement and anticipation for the day Leslie finds out that she is pregnant again.

Because God has seen fit to have us wait, the value of children has skyrocketed in our eyes. In fact, the longer we wait, the more anticipation we have for another little bundle of life. If you were to talk with Leslie and me about children, we would say, "Those cute little critters are not something to ever take for granted. And they must always be cherished, adored, and slobbered over with delight."

I used to be scared spitless about having a little baby, but Sacred has taught me to cherish the things God declares to be precious to Him. I absolutely love little children now. And this is just one of the many amazing results of sacred waiting.

Sacred Waiting Opportunity #2: Waiting to Serve. Leslie and I feel strongly that God is calling us to add a new element to our ministry: serving the poor. As Christ Himself did—to get away from our comforts, bend our knee in sacrifice, and pour out our lives in service of those in need. It's a fantastic, even romantic vision, and it stirs the deepest embers of our souls, but God has us in a period of "sacred waiting."

We know there will soon be a new dimension to our ministry, but we don't yet know where or how it's going to happen. Whereas, this could prove rather frustrating, it has instead proven to be a sacred work of beauty and romance. We aren't sure if our opportunities are right down the road or overseas; that is why we are studying every country, every people, and therefore, praying for every country and every people. We are learning to love the world just as Jesus does. It is extraordinary, and it is the result of sacred waiting.

Sacred Waiting Opportunity #3: Waiting for Spring. The forty-nine days that Sacred tested me during the writing of this book were the forty-nine coldest days in Colorado history, with the most snowfall since 1914. "I thought Punxsutawney Phil saw his shadow this year," Leslie muttered more than a few times over those weeks. "Doesn't that mean we are supposed to have an early spring?" Even in the area of weather, Sacred was testing us, teaching us to anticipate.

Leslie, Hudson, and I have all been sick multiple times throughout these past seven weeks. But a sore throat, a hacking cough, and a runny nose haven't stopped us from having the time of our lives with each other. Sacred has been teaching us to appreciate every minute of our lives together and to never take for granted the beauty of family, of marriage, and of friendships.

So even with this unusually arctic weather, we have been seeing the beauty of what "sacred waiting" can produce. We certainly will never take for granted spring, summer, and fall ever again.

◻ ◻ ◻

These three things, just mentioned, are by no means the only things for which Leslie and I have been waiting. There are ten, maybe even twenty little things in our lives that Sacred is constantly using to train us in the refined art of appreciation through the discipline of sacred waiting.

But the most beautiful thing Sacred has done during these past seven weeks while I have been waiting for the next blue sticky note from the League is in regard to my marriage with Leslie. Sacred has driven into the core of my understanding how precious and how rare what I share with Leslie really is. And she has caused me to slow down and fully appreciate what I do have so that I will take care of it with more attentiveness, more thoughtfulness, and more tenderness than I ever have before.

When I surrendered this book to Sacred, the first thing she nudged me to do was set aside the book and learn to love Leslie better than I've ever loved her before. Sacred was indirectly saying, "Peeps, I want to show you how to move beyond the beginner's level. Your relationship with Leslie is more valuable than this book. And you can only advance with Great Sex as far as your value system aligns with God's value system. So give yourself wholly to time with Leslie and I guarantee you that you will have more than enough material to fill this little book of yours on Great Sex. And maybe you will even begin to move beyond being classified as just a beginner."

My life should never be described as, "Oh, Eric Ludy, he's that guy who writes *about* Great Love and Great Sex." Rather, it should be described as, "Oh, Eric Ludy, isn't he that supremely happy dude who experiences Great Love and Great Sex in an ever-increasing measure in his life and marriage every day?" This is what Sacred has reminded me about over these past forty-nine days. By stripping me of the ability to write on this book, she turned my heart toward the great sacred treasure sleeping next to me every night.

This book, probably to your surprise, is not as much for you as it is for me. I thought I had it good in my marriage when I picked up a pen and began to write this manuscript. But in this journey toward interviewing Great Sex, I have realized that I haven't even begun to become Mr. Marvelous. But you can bet I'm headed full-steam in that direction. And it won't be just Leslie who is going to appreciate it when that title is finally earned.

Sacred needs access to each one of us. And you can be certain, when she starts her work it will inevitably involve some "relinquishment," some "waiting," and some serious amounts of "sacred choreography." Sacred desires to set your life apart from all the mediocre lives about you and make you look, act, and experience life completely different from the pack. Sacred desires to give you a different quality of life and, therefore, she will need to work on you in a way that may seem strange and uncomfortable at first. But the end result is an entirely supernatural level of satisfaction and joy.

When everyone else is taking their sexuality and giving it to the dogs, Sacred desires to teach us how to guard it and appreciate it for its proper and perfect use.

From personal experience I can assure you, every time I allow Mr. Purity and Sacred to do their work in my soul, I emerge from the test happier, healthier, and ready to shout from the mountaintops.

A Step Further

In the back of this book, appendix B to be precise, Leslie and I have provided you with some practical thoughts on how you can apply these sacred truths to your personal life today. If you don't wish to chew on these "meaty" thoughts now, then feel free to check them out later when you are ready to do a little spiritual exercising.

CHAPTER 13

Mr. Marvelous

When 10:00 a.m. arrived, I was sitting expectantly at a table near the back of Cup of Loodles Café, sipping from a ceramic mug filled with hot chai and scanning the room for Sacred. I had printed out my manuscript for Mr. Purity and Sacred to read, and I had a general giddiness about me. After all, it had been forty-nine days.

The front door jangled open, but to my disappointment, two businessmen strolled in, chatting about coffee futures.

Another few minutes passed and the door remained shut. It was odd for members of the League to be late. Their timing was always perfect—never early, never late.

When I reached down to grab the handle of my ceramic mug, I noticed a blue sticky note sitting on top of my printed manuscript. As I read it, I couldn't suppress a smile.

Peeps! Waiting always increases the anticipation, doesn't it? Never fear, we will be there at the perfect time.

I read the note a couple more times, trying to figure out how it got there without my knowing.

I spent a few more minutes polishing off the remaining tasty treasure inside that ceramic mug and realized how similar this felt to when Leslie and I were falling in love and waiting to be married. It was the same tension of soul, the same longing to press forward, and the same sacred guard whispering to my heart, *Be patient, Eric. All in God's perfect timing.*

I decided to steal a piece of paper from my writing notepad and jot a quick love note to Leslie:

Dearest Love,

I appreciate you now more than ever. The years have done nothing to dull our love; rather, it has only increased its strength, resolve, depth, richness, and intensity. You are more beautiful, more enchanting, more fascinating, and more magnetic to my heart than ever, and time spent with you reminds me of time spent with my heavenly King.

I'm currently waiting at Loodles to meet with Sacred. I can't tell you how excited I am to see what is next in this great adventure called love. Thank you for putting up with me for so long as Mr. Mediocre. It is my great desire to treat you, my lady, to the very best version of masculinity this world has ever seen. Since Jesus is the only man who has ever really done this manhood thing right, it is my prayer and my active pursuit to become a miniature replica of Him for you, my Love, my enchanting and supremely marvelous bride. So brace yourself, dear princess of my heart—here comes Mr. Marvelous!

With a triple helping of mush,
Your beloved Beef

I share that love note with you now, even at risk of making some of you yell, "Get a room!" simply because the irony of what took place next would be lost if I didn't. For it was at the very moment in which I finished penning that love note, having waxed eloquently about the coming of Mr. Marvelous, that I looked up, and before me sat a man. But this wasn't just any man. This was a man among men. If Jesus is termed the King of kings, this guy would be termed the Dude of dudes, the Stud of studs, or the Guy of guys. And I knew instantaneously who this was. *It was Mr. Marvelous.*

"Mr. Marvelous, I presume?" I said, feeling a surge of adrenaline shoot through my veins.

"At your service, Mr. Ludy," he said with a bow of his handsome head.

Wow! I thought. There are very few things that take a man's breath away with admiration, but magnificent, warrior-poet masculinity is one of them.

"Would you mind, Mr. Ludy," Marvelous asked politely, "if we pull up a couple of chairs for my friends?"

There behind me stood the hulking figure of Purity and the graceful form of Sacred. We yanked up two more chairs, the three of us men standing until Sacred took her seat.

"Kudos, Peeps! You're getting the hang of it!" Sacred said to me with a wink.

I sat down with excitement pumping through my body. My ceramic mug was empty, leaving me little to fidget with but my pen as I attempted to digest this extraordinary scene unfolding about me. I was in an intimate conference with three of the world's greatest superheroes. I couldn't wait to go home and tell Leslie all about this.

Mr. Marvelous cleared his throat and calmly stated, "Mr. Ludy, I wish to thank you for your many years of honorable support of my stalwart mission to bring back magnificent manhood."

I nodded and swallowed hard, attempting to get my tongue to start working.

"You truly have been my Edwin," the manly man said with deep sincerity in his voice.

Reader, I realize that may mean absolutely nothing to you. You may be wondering, "Who the wang-do is Edwin?" But, for a guy who has read and reread and reread *The Scottish Chiefs* and has longed to be like William Wallace, to be told that I am an Edwin is the next best thing to someone saying to me, "William Wallace, is that you?"

Edwin Ruthven was young and still a bit green in his manhood, but he was noble, brave, and the dearest confidante of Sir William Wallace. Edwin was a William Wallace in the making, an up-and-coming warrior-poet. So for this überman to refer to me in this manner was like a shot of pure testosterone into my bloodstream.

As I observed these three heroic characters, I couldn't help feeling like I wanted to bottle this scene and never let it expire. Mr. Purity, Sacred, and Mr. Marvelous all blended together were the essence of what I desired my life to be.

"Well now," said Mr. Purity when he realized that my ability to speak was impaired, "to be called an Edwin is not too shabby, Mr. Ludy. I'd consider that a mighty high compliment if I were you."

I nodded my agreement and let out a nervous and awkward laugh, attempting to make myself appear loose.

"So," Sacred said, "what did you think about my seven-week test?"

I smiled. "It was forty-nine days of heaven," I said, much appreciative of the change of topic.

"Tell me," she said giddily, "what was your favorite part?"

"That's a difficult one," I said stroking my chin. "Obviously what you taught me about the even greater degrees of cherishing my wife was spectacular, and I would hate to ever downplay how extraordinary that was, but . . ."

"But?" she prompted.

"I honestly would have to say, it was what the testing time did in my relationship, admiration, and passion for Christ that was my favorite part."

"That's what I love to hear," responded Sacred proudly. "I love to help couples find Great Sex, but it's my great passion to help them find the treasure of satisfying intimacy with Jesus Christ more than anything."

"Well, you sure are good at it!"

"I know I said this to you in the beginning, Mr. Ludy," interjected Mr. Purity, "but I hope you remember to put heavy emphasis on this point in your writing." The massive man leaned in and spoke with utter seriousness, "The work we do in this League is not just so that you, or anyone else, can find Great Sex—it's so you can find the fullness of a life shared with Jesus Christ. Great Sex is merely an earthly taste of something truly heavenly that every human is designed to share with the Almighty."

"I'll be sure to communicate that clearly," I said to Mr. Purity.

"You'd better, or I'll pull the plug on this process right here and right now!"

It was fun to see Mr. Purity huffing and puffing and getting defensive for the work of Jesus Christ. I love how seriously he takes his job. And I love how he wants me to take his job just as seriously as he does.

Sacred patted her man on his shoulder and said, "I think we can trust him, dear!"

"Well, I'll be watching you!" he said, not quite satisfied that I'd gotten the point.

"Oh, I have no doubt you will," I chuckled.

There was a lull in the conversation until Mr. Marvelous started it back up. "Well, Mr. Ludy," he said, "it's an honor to finally meet face-to-face."

"It's my honor, sir," I said, realizing that my nerves had become settled enough for me to discourse with this man.

"I read your book about manhood, *God's Gift to Women*," he said with a smile. "Quite the appropriate title, I might add."

"Uh, yeah," I winced, feeling like an idiot that this guy had read my ramblings.

"However," he frowned, "you were off-base on one very critical point, Mr. Ludy."

My heart sunk with embarrassment as I prepared myself to listen to his critique.

"You didn't aim high enough, young man. You are still too young to understand this, but God's purposes for manhood go far beyond even what you described!"

My eyes were wide with amazement. In the course of the past couple of months I had discovered that I was both a beginner at Great Sex and aiming too low in my vision for manhood. Ironically, I could not possibly imagine how Sex could get any better and I couldn't imagine a version of manhood any loftier than what I had described in that book.

"And yet," Mr. Marvelous continued, "your humble little book was, all in all, rather complimentary to my work."

"I'm very glad to hear that," I said, swallowing hard.

I reached under the table and placed my hand firmly on my knee to try to stop its shaking. I was as nervous as an eight-year-old in the dentist's chair.

I looked up at Mr. Marvelous with a quizzical gaze and asked an awkward question. "Are you . . . um . . . are you Jesus?"

The handsome man laughed heartily, accompanied by the chuckles of Mr. Purity and Sacred.

"No! No!" he smiled kindly. "But don't feel bad. I get that a lot. The King certainly uses me as one of His primary tools in expressing His love. But no, I'm not God; I'm just a picture of what God is capable of doing in a man."

All I could think was, *If this isn't Jesus Christ, then wow, wow, wow! Jesus must be something to behold!*

Mr. Marvelous was not as big a man as Mr. Purity, but in no

way did his smaller stature lessen his manly presence. Mr. Marvelous was visibly strong and capable, though his virtue wasn't found in his strength but in his grace. He carried a solemn dignity, a holy charm. My first impression of him was noticing what he seemed to *not* possess. He had no self-awareness, no self-conceit, no self-protectiveness, and not even a hint of sexual pollution. In my thirty-six years, I don't think I have ever before seen a man without at least a vague crust of self-consideration about his life. This man was wholly unique, wholly extraordinary, and wholly impressive.

Even though it was the absence of certain qualities that caught my fascination first, as the conversation progressed, it was the presence of certain attributes that ultimately forced me to say to myself, "I want everything this guy's got!"

I later told Leslie that I felt like the Bible was on display in front of me. As he interacted with Mr. Purity, Sacred, and me, I saw evidence of Christ that was thoroughly exhilarating to witness. Mr. Marvelous knew Mr. Purity so intimately that it was as if he could read the hulking bodyguard's every thought. He could have finished his sentences if he wished, but he was much too courteous to do so.

And I was mesmerized with how Marvelous related to Sacred. He treated her as if every movement she made was significant, every sound she uttered was precious, and as if every glance of her eye should be followed and its object wholly appreciated. It was as if she controlled him, and the passion of those hundred puppy dogs that yipped within her dwelt within his soul as well, as a result of their unique bond.

He was kind. So kind in fact that I felt he was vulnerable of being taken advantage of.

He was courteous. But it was a rare sort of courtesy. It went beyond gentlemanly honor and found expression in that rare princely grace known as sacred honor.

He was noble—the kind of nobility that causes you to think he possessed the pedigree of ancient kings. He was of a gallant, honorable, and heroic bloodline—magnanimous, chivalrous, and marked with a sublime dignity.

He was courage personified, bravery brought to life. His square jaw and his frock of chestnut hair certainly lent him a classic attractiveness, but it was his grand smile that amazed me. He was utterly satisfied in life, completely happy, possessing not the slightest trace of darkness in his sunny disposition.

He was a poet with his every word spoken. An artist with encouragement, a musician with his praise and adoration of his King, and a skilled artisan with his ability to make everyone about him seem important and included in the conversation.

"Mr. Purity," he said at one point, "I've known you for years, my friend, but I never cease to be amazed at your observation skills and your ability to root the mole out of the soul's garden."

Then at another point, he leaned over and said sweetly to Sacred, "You make every room a brighter room, dear sister!"

As I observed Mr. Marvelous, I wanted it all—from his square jaw and chestnut hair to his poetic words and courageous heart. Why not? Just throw it all in. Leslie deserved better than me; she deserved Mr. Marvelous! She deserved a perfected, Christ-built man.

"You may not be a finished piece of art, Mr. Ludy," he said, seeming to be reading my thoughts, "but never lose the hope that what Christ has begun to build in your masculinity, He will also complete."

"But Leslie deserves a man like you. I'm just a wannabe!"

Mr. Marvelous chuckled in amusement. "Being a 'wannabe' is what this life is all about. Everything good that flows out of life flows out of being a wannabe. You must want to be like Jesus, Mr. Ludy, to realize how unlike Him you actually are. Then you must want to be like Jesus so much that you give up everything in order to receive the impartation of His Spirit-life into your body. And finally, you must want to be with Him so desperately that you spend every moment of your existence abiding in His loving, joyful, peaceful presence. Yes, you are a wannabe, Mr. Ludy, and that is precisely why you will find what you are after."

"Can I be a man like you?"

"You may never have my biceps, my square jaw, or my chestnut brown hair, if that is what you mean." He smiled, eyeing my golfer's physique. "But you can have every last quality I possess, if you allow Mr. Purity and Sacred to build the pattern of my manhood into your existence."

My interview with Mr. Marvelous lasted nearly two hours, and as far as I was concerned, it could have lasted two years. The man was a picture of everything I respected, loved, honored, and desired to become. He was strong yet sensitive, bold yet humble, courageous yet compassionate.

Somewhere around the seventy-minute juncture, I remembered that I was writing a book to introduce Great Sex. I was almost disappointed, because I wanted to continue in our conversational direction. We had been talking about manly valor and how such valor expresses itself in delivering the gospel to this world. Mr. Marvelous's comments were both inspiring and deeply convicting, yet due to the need to move on in this book,

I will have to detail his thoughts on the matter to you at a different time.

When I asked him about his role in Great Sex, he paused, looked at me with an ever-widening grin, and laughed uproariously. The chorus of laughter was excruciatingly difficult to bear, for it was both uncomfortably loud as well as emanating from every chair around the table. My question obviously was a funny one.

"Do you wish for me to share with you about the birds and the bees, Peeps?" Sacred whispered in my ear.

"We just figured you already knew . . ." Purity chuckled.

"OK, that's enough!" I spouted with an understanding smile. "I didn't mean how a man's physical body mechanically is supposed to work in Sex. I was wondering . . ."

"Don't worry, my friend, we know exactly what you meant." Mr. Marvelous once again proved exceedingly gracious. "Forgive us enjoying a little laughter whenever it can be afforded."

"Take it as a compliment, Peeps," Sacred said with a grin. "We know you are strong enough for us to poke fun at you."

"So," said Mr. Marvelous, "thank you for allowing us to enjoy a little levity amid our sacred, solemn duties."

"I give you full permission," I said, "to laugh as often as you want when around me. It's contagious!"

The next hour was full of questions and answers. It was exhilarating! I felt like a little kid on a shopping spree inside Al's Toy Barn. I absolutely love the topic of manhood. And after spending two hours with Mr. Marvelous, I can honestly say I'm even more motivated about the topic than ever before.

Meeting Mr. Marvelous leaves you stunned. As a guy you think, *If that's what God desires to craft me into—I'm ready! Do it!*

Start today! As a girl, you think, *If I'm going to get married, I want a guy just like him!*

When the door of Loodles jangled at the exiting of Mr. Marvelous, Sacred, and Purity, I sat in silence for a while, just staring at my empty ceramic mug. Then when my wits began to slowly return, I grabbed my pen and wrote Leslie another letter. But this letter was unlike any I had ever written to her before.

In this next chapter, you will read the letter that I wrote to her. I wish every one of you could have been present to listen to Mr. Marvelous talk. It was life altering. And I have struggled to discern how best to share with you the contents of our conversation. I believe that sharing with you the letter I wrote to Leslie immediately following the interview is probably the single most effective means of transmitting the grandeur of those two hours into your hearts and minds.

I have titled the following letter, "Confessions of an Unmarvelous Man."

CHAPTER 14

Dearest Leslie

Cup of Loodles Café
February 14, 2007
Valentine's Day

Dearest Leslie,

Part of me wishes to run home to you right now, wrap my arms around you, squeeze you until you squeal, and kiss your lips as if they were chocolate morsels. But I realize that what is stirring inside of me needs to work its way a bit deeper before I begin to speak it, or shout it, or even sing it. For it is a wonderful thing and it deserves to be brought forth with grandeur and not merely gush. So I will first attempt to write it.

I have guzzled four very large ceramic mugs full of chai these past two hours. Thanks may be given to our good friend Deuce for his attentiveness to my seeming unquenchable thirst. But as a result, I find myself a bit jittery with the caffeine and not knowing if what is transpiring in my heart currently is the work of extreme Spirit-enthusiasm or 220 volts of caffeine stirring in my belly. Either way, I'm thrilled to be alive, and so grateful to our ever-generous and gracious God for giving me the life He has. I am especially thankful for you.

I know I speak these words to you every day, but I wish to say them afresh right now. I want you to listen to these words as if all heaven has stopped to listen in and a chorus of the angelic host is singing softly in the background to make it the perfect cinematic moment. Imagine that these words, even though they hold the identical audio echo as they have always held, somehow have a power to be truer now than they have ever been before. Imagine I take your hand, kneel before you just as I did when I proposed to you nearly thirteen years ago, and whisper with an emotion-laden frog stuck in my larynx, "My girl Leslie, I love you! I love you so much it hurts!"

I have never been a husband to stifle words of adoration, but I realize that I should be gushing my affections for you a hundred, if not a thousand times more often than I currently do. And why shouldn't I? Why should I settle for telling you five times a day that you are precious when I could be proclaiming it fifty-five times? And why should I kiss you seven times a day when I could be kissing you seventy-seven? I wish to love you to the absolute extent that an earthly man is capable of loving his earthly wife—fully, wholly, with abandon, with eagerness, and with flair.

As I write this, Deuce has once again filled my ceramic mug to the top. In a way that is almost a metaphor for what this day has been for me. Every time I think I've finished drinking in the full and complete glory of God, believing that I've finally reached the end of God's beauty and brilliance, my cup is filled again with a fresh revelation that I have only just begun to sip at the ocean of heavenly chai that God has for His children.

I wished so many times that you had been sitting at this small table with me at 10:12 this morning. It wasn't just that I missed you—which I did. But I wished that you could share it all with me, next to me. And I wish I could just look at you right now and say, "Wow!" and have you know precisely what I mean. But since you weren't there, I'm forced to try to pass it on, and deliver something in mere words that I encountered in actual presence. I saw the intensity in his eyes, the love within his smile, the streak of silver in his chestnut brown hair—but I can only use mere words of humble description to speak of them to you.

He was amazing! I saw manhood the way God intended it to be. I thought I already possessed a supremely grand vision of masculinity, but what I saw today made me feel wholly green in my manly maturity and wholly unmarvelous in my masculine progress thus far. He spoke to me, Leslie. His voice was kind and yet weighty with the unction of God's Spirit. He told me that I was his Edwin. He knew precisely what I needed to hear and he spoke it with gentleness and truthfulness. As he spoke, it was as if he dressed me in his nobility. I'm struggling to know how he did it, but it was as if he allowed me to feel as if I, too, shared his dignity and possessed a high degree of honor. I felt like I was in the sacred corridors of the royal court and the king was treating me as an equal. It was a marvelous feeling, a feeling of being important and highly esteemed. And however he did this, he did it naturally without the slightest degree of effort. I wish to be such a man!

He was utterly pure! I have never seen anything quite like it, my love. I realized that Mr. Purity has only just begun with me, for as I watched this grand picture of manhood, I realized that the possibilities and potentials of moral strength and of inward excellence are just as vast as the Milky Way galaxy. To watch him interact with Mr. Purity was breathtaking. They seemed to know each other and anticipate each other at every turn of the conversation. If Mr. Purity ever thought something, then Mr. Marvelous thought it too. It was uncanny and truly beautiful to witness.

He was holy! Sacred had a control over his life that proved one of the most glorious displays of heaven on earth that I have ever seen. He was not his own. He had no agenda of his own. His words were chosen for him, and they were like muscular poetry. His actions were choreographed by someone else, and they were full of gracious love and soul-quickening kindness. Sacred held in her possession his eyes, his tongue, his ears, his hands, his feet, his appetite, and his heart. This marvelous man was not his own, but bought with a price, and his existence was directed by the Spirit of Holiness, orchestrated by Sacred's musical hand. And his life was stronger than strong and yet more supple than supple—it was everything I've ever said Christ-built warrior-poet manhood could be, and a thousand times more.

Mr. Marvelous taught me so much today, dearest Leslie. He taught me how to present a more superior brand of love in our marriage. He taught me how to bring you to life, how to listen to you better, how to hear your silent voice speaking in addition to hearing your spoken voice. He taught me a host of exciting things that I can't wait to apply in our marriage, but there was one thing he spoke to me that absolutely hushed my soul and brought me into the inner courts of kingly grace. He said, "Mr. Ludy, a truly great man must pick up his cross daily and die for his girl. Yes, you must die for Christ, but you must also relinquish everything for your girl, the same way Jesus relinquished everything for His Bride!"

The context for that statement ironically was Great Sex. He was introducing me to the attitude of a heroic man in the bedroom. But his truth resonated in every sector of my life and soul. In many ways, I may give up my life for Jesus theoretically but fail to give up my life for you practically. But great manhood is demanding more of me. It demands that I take the head position. And as the head I take the responsibility for everything that enters our home, our marriage, and our ministry. As the head I am the one who should take the hits that life inevitably doles out in order to love you and little Hudson the way Christ loves His Bride. I must be willing to initiate forgiveness after every quarrel, initiate spiritual growth at every turn in life's road, initiate prayer as many times a day and for as long each day as God would lead. I must be available to God's voice and to your voice always. When you need a listening ear, a manly prayer of strength, a word of husband comfort, or even a really long hug and forty-five minutes of togetherness—I long to be there, ready, and armed with tenderness for whatever your heart needs.

Mr. Marvelous prodded me today. He shook all the dust of remaining apathy off my manly soul and ushered me into an entirely new dimension of masculinity—sold-out masculinity, cross-bearing masculinity, purity-loving masculinity, holiness-choreographed masculinity, love-inspired masculinity, and selfless-wholly-given-over-to-the-control-of-God's-gracious-Spirit masculinity.

I confess that I am still a very unmarvelous man. But I sense that Mr. Marvelous has begun to work within my life at an even greater degree than he ever has before. As he spoke today, I felt iron forming within my spine and holy testosterone charging through my veins. I confess, dearest Leslie, that I am not a full expression of Jesus Christ on planet earth, but His Spirit possesses me, and today I witnessed what the Almighty wishes to do in and through my masculine nature. I confess that I cannot love you with such a perfect love as Christ's without help. But I am confident that as I move to love you in such a heavenly way, God will supply that heavenly deposit of love to pour through me and unto you. I confess to being unmarvelous now, but I refuse to remain where I am today.

Just think, Leslie. If our love story is grand and glorious now with me petering along at the beginner's level in both Great Sex and Manhood—what's it going to be like when I begin to catch the hang of all this?

We decided when we were first married that every day would be Valentine's Day. But even though we've always said that Valentine's Day to us is of no greater significance than any other beautiful romance-filled day, if you would allow me, precious wife, I wish to edit our previous statements on the matter. Sacred gave me a forty-nine day test and she chose today to end it. I think that means that this day IS special. It is the day I learned how to love you even better. It is the day that I met and interviewed Mr. Marvelous.

So I say, let's celebrate our love today. And even though every restaurant will be booked and every rose will cost four times the usual amount—I don't care! I just want to cherish our love and not wait a moment longer to become a more marvelous man just for you.

Cherishing everything about you,
Your Loverboy

A Step Further

Check out appendix C for some additional testosterone-infused thoughts on great manhood and see how you can begin to practically integrate these *marvelous* ideas into your own life, attitude, and relationships. Whether you are a guy or girl, I believe you will find these ideas very inspiring!

CHAPTER 15

My Darling Beef

The Coffee Grounds
February 14, 2007
Valentine's Day

My Darling Beef,

I realize that when you return from Loodles today you will be anxious to tell me all. And I wish you to know, my love, that I am so excited to hear it—every last detail of your amazing day. But for reasons that will soon be very clear, I am away. Don't worry, Hudson is spending time at cousin Dash's house, and very satisfied with the vast selection of new toys with which he is free to play. I presently am at The Coffee Grounds in Fort Collins.

You see, when you left this morning, I found a blue sticky note on my computer monitor. It simply read, *Coffee*

Grounds, North College Avenue, 12:00. Eric must be surprised.

The handwriting matched that of the previous blue sticky notes that you keep posted above your writing desk, so I made arrangements for Hudson and ventured northward to the Coffee Grounds.

Mr. Purity greeted me at the door. You said he was large, but Beefy dear, this man is much more than large. As I strolled into the little café, I felt like a tiny mouse in the shadow of a woolly mammoth. But though he is a bit daunting to look at, he is a pleasant and kind man, isn't he?

He led me to a small sitting area in the rear of the dimly lit café, where there were two elegant and exquisite women awaiting my arrival. You know I've always dreamed of playing a role in a Jane Austen novel, and this seemed to be my golden moment. As I entered their sanctuary, the two ladies stood and greeted me as if I were Elizabeth Bennet entering the Pemberley estate for tea. I felt fully feminine, and a surge of breathless joy seemed to fill my soul.

I recognized Sacred instantly and, as strange as this might sound, wished to give her a kiss. I've really never been the kissing kind of girl, so I fumbled a bit as I approached her, and then, seeing my hesitation, she gently leaned in, kissed my cheek, and whispered, "You needn't ever hesitate to embrace me, dear Leslie." It was an extraordinary and an entirely unusual experience. From that very first moment, I simply marveled at her presence, her life, and at those "hundred puppy dogs" you had told me about that really do seem to frolic about inside her heart and burst forth with holy love in and through her eyes, her smile, and her every word.

But, dearest Beefy, it wasn't so that I could meet Mr. Purity and Sacred that I was called here today. It was so that I might be formally introduced to someone new, someone you haven't yet had the privilege to meet.

I hope this doesn't spoil your surprise, but I know that you met with Mr. Marvelous earlier this day. Mr. Purity described to me a few bits of your conversation, and I know that it must have been a holy moment when he greeted you and called you his "Edwin." My eyes filled with tears when I first heard it as well as they do now as I reminisce and write it on this stationery. How precious. I'm so proud of you.

I know you have so much to share. But first, I must share something with you. Something has just transpired in my life that is similar to your euphoric encounter; for after you met Mr. Marvelous, I was brought into the presence of the most perfected demonstration of femininity. After Sacred whispered into my ear, she took my hand and placed it gently in the delicate but strong hand of an angel. I've actually never seen an angel, so I'm not sure if this is what an angel looks like, but "angel" is the most beautiful, strong, yet delicate word I can think to describe such a picture. She was elegant, royal, mysterious, and seemed to squeeze Sacred's hand as if drawing some unseen power out of her dear attendant's embrace.

She was Feminine Grace.

You know how I love words, but I am at a loss in trying to describe her majesty. She was Audrey Hepburn meets Amy Carmichael. She was dignity meets devotion, winsome radiance meets holy abandon. She was elegant mystique meets poured-out love. She was noble yet nurturing, regal yet real, so far above me and yet treated me as if I were the first lady of the kingdom. She was everything I want to be yet everything it seems like I'm so far from ever becoming.

Remember how I said to you the other day that I wish to have Gladys Aylward's abandon, Joan of Arc's courage, and Amy Carmichael's grit? Well, she was all this and more. She wasn't merely soft and fragile femininity; she was also the bold and daring femininity I've been longing to see cultivated within me.

Beef, I'm writing this letter between meetings. Sacred informed me that there was still yet another meeting scheduled for this afternoon. I asked if you would be present at this next meeting, and she answered mysteriously, "Come and find out, my dear."

Everything has happened so quickly that I fear I'm not fully absorbing the glory of this occasion. After my meeting with Feminine Grace was concluded, Sacred set this stationery in front of me along with a fountain pen and simply said, "Please write to your husband, Leslie dear, and tell him what has just transpired."

How this letter will reach you, I don't pretend to know,

but I'm confident it will somehow get to you, by heavenly courier no less.

I asked Sacred if she wished me to tell you anything about the upcoming meeting. "Tell him that the long-awaited encounter with Mr. Smith awaits," she responded coyly.

I'm sorry, precious husband, that I must be so vague. Sacred is an artist with romance, so I fully trust her in this. I know you have been waiting twelve long weeks to gain an interview with Great Sex. I don't know who Mr. Smith is, but maybe meeting with him will at least bring us one step closer.

I hope you won't be too upset that I've entered into your portion of the book. I didn't mean for this to happen. But it does make sense that you would meet with Mr. Marvelous and that *I* would meet with Feminine Grace. After all, Beefy dear, it does take two to tango in this lovely thing known as Great Sex. And if Great Sex is going to be found, it seems only right that both of us would be a part of it. So I will not apologize for the fact that God designed this process to involve me. In fact, I am excited to know that you need me along this journey.

Beef, I thought of you and Jesus the entire time Feminine Grace was talking. She was beyond lovely, yet I wasn't bewitched by her beauty, but rather, strangely drawn closer to Jesus and to you with her every comment. I wish to learn her secrets—all of them. She actually caused me to love you and appreciate you even more.

She seemed to glow every time she even mentioned the idea of manhood. As I saw her gently touch Mr. Purity on the arm and say, "Thank you, dear friend, for being such a protector," I wished to reach out my hand and gently touch you and say the very same words. I don't say those words enough. But I wish to. I wish to honor you not merely with my every word spoken, but with my every thought. Oh, I ache to be a better wife, a clearer picture of Christ's love to you.

Feminine Grace said something to me that I dare not ever forget. "Sweet Leslie," she said, "let your husband be as Jesus to you." She smiled so kindly, so lovingly, and added, "Love him so well, so fiercely, so heartily as if he were Christ and you were Mary of Bethany at his feet."

Her words were like a clap of thunder to my heart. I have loved you, Beef, but I've fallen short of loving so completely as that. I've never given myself so fully in love as to risk my dignity. But as she spoke I realized that such adoration and givenness is the essence of feminine beauty—it is poured-out perfume unto a Bridegroom, elegant abandon unto a Prince, graceful vulnerability before my chosen man—first to Jesus, and then to you.

It's beautiful, isn't it? And I wish for more of such sacred beauty in our love story.

You might think that to encounter the perfection of Feminine Grace might cause me to feel I am a horrid, dirty, and miserable failure—but quite to the contrary, I feel quickened by the grace of God to grow more and more every day, from here on, into such a splendid image of beauty.

Forgive me, dearest Beefy, for the many days I chose not to progress toward such perfection and I stewed in my own selfish haze convincing myself that I had journeyed far enough in regard to femininity. I honestly wonder if I have even begun, let alone gone "far enough."

When we woke up this morning, I totally forgot it was Valentine's Day. Please forgive me. It's just that you kissed me on the lips at five in the morning and startled me out of my dream world. I guess my brain wasn't fully operational yet. But come to think of it, you never mentioned anything about Valentine's Day either. So I guess you owe me an apology too.

I realize that in the past we have sort of snickered at the thought of celebrating our love on this day, seeing as how everyone seems to deem it the only day of the year on which to be romantic. However, I wish for us to revisit our sentiments. For it seems that God Himself is saying, "Today is special!" I adore the fact that you are committed to making every day a day for celebrating our love, but let us not celebrate 364 days and risk forgetting today.

I hope you are ready to do some serious kissing. Because I am in desperate need of one of your patented princely kisses. I want you to pick me up and swing me around and whisper your affections into my ear. And please don't forget, when you set me back down, to take your right hand and run it tenderly through my dark brown locks and say, with your sweetest, most gentle voice, "You are truly lovely!"

And never fear, my dear Mr. Marvelous, I will respond with the truest feminine desire as if I had been waiting in the apex of a grand tower for a hundred years and have ached for my Prince Charming to finally arrive and rescue me.

You are the man I love, Mr. Ludy. You are the man I have chosen and covenanted my life to. And I dare say, I have impeccable taste in men, for you are a rare and treasured variety of masculinity. I only hope that I can be a woman worthy of such a man as you.

Your blushing bride,
Leslie

A Step Further

Check out appendix D for additional perfumed-thoughts about true femininity and how you can practically integrate the beauty and grace of heaven into this all-important arena of life and love. Again, these thoughts are very inspiring for male and female alike!

CHAPTER 16

Mr. Smith

I walked in through the front door of our house at approximately 1:05 on Valentine's Day afternoon. I held in my right hand a bouquet of white lilies, and an enthusiasm swarmed within my chest. I was a very motivated man in desperate need of a kiss from my bride.

I called for Leslie, but to no avail. She obviously wasn't home, so I ventured into the kitchen in order to find a more permanent home for the flowers clenched within my fist. It was there on the corner of the kitchen counter that I saw Leslie's letter. It was folded and clothed in a soft plum, vellum envelope that simply read, "Beef" on the outside. There was a sprig of lavender beside it and a sense of romance hovering over it.

I cherish love letters from my wife. In fact, in our marriage, the writing and giving of love letters is a very noble and elegant process. It would be easier and faster to write e-mails to each other that contain expressions of affection, but somewhere along the line we decided to start making the process of expressing our love more dignified and even more beautiful. As I did in my single days, we started writing love letters by hand, on beautiful stationery, encased in lovely accouterments, and then given with romantic finesse.

I picked up the soft plum envelope and carried it into our reading room by the hearth. I carefully cracked its seal and pulled from the vellum envelope the multiple pages of fine lilac-colored paper.

What I read at that sitting was precisely what you just read in chapter 15. Leslie's letter was such a perfect enunciation of Christ-shaped femininity. I was mystified and entranced by her words. To think, the final two superheroes in the League were none other than True Manhood and True Femininity. Of course, it made total sense. I was just shocked that I hadn't seen this before. I was moved deeply by the beauty of it all. A smile curled upon my face as I envisioned Mr. Purity and Sacred building this entire drama, with all their secrets, their mystery, and their romantic panache.

As I concluded the letter, reading, "Your blushing bride, Leslie," I realized that there was still another piece of stationery included in the letter. When I looked at it, there, stuck to its face, was a blue sticky note that stated the following: *Your attendance is requested. Mr. Smith awaits. Follow blue Pontiac to meeting place.*

Mr. Smith? I thought to myself. *Who the wang-do is Mr. Smith?*

I stood up and looked outside into the street. Sure enough, there sat a blue Pontiac with tinted windows and the engine running.

□ □ □

The drive to meet this Mr. Smith was a circuitous adventure that lasted exactly sixty-seven minutes. I had filled up my gas tank on the way to Loodles Café that morning, so I was providentially prepared for this journey up the side of a high mountain, down the other side, over a rickety wooden bridge, and then through a forest of evergreens. Somewhere amid the dense evergreen canopy, the blue Pontiac came to a stop and I pulled in behind it.

This was fun! I was laughing to myself as I turned my engine off. Here I was attempting to write a book about Great Sex, and no matter how hard I tried to be the one writing it, someone else seemed to be scripting the adventure.

This place was out of a storybook. I could see Sacred outside strewing a blanket of rose petals all over the ground. Just a hundred feet straight ahead there was an opening in the pines that revealed a majestic view of the white-capped Rocky Mountains. And there to my left, Mr. Purity was sweeping the front porch of a little mountain cottage. Mr. Marvelous was carrying a hefty stack of firewood and there, to my right, stepping out of the blue Pontiac was none other than Feminine Grace—the essence of perfected womanhood. Leslie had described her well. She was enchanting. I was almost convinced that I was staring at Leslie, but this wasn't Leslie. She looked over at me and smiled warmly, inviting me to join the festivities.

"What is this place?" I muttered to myself in bewilderment. I exited from my car with a sense of awe hovering about my heart like a thick cloud.

"Welcome, Peeps!" Sacred said with a smile as I approached the small chalet.

The soles of my winter boots crunched into the snow as well as into Sacred's carpet of roses.

"What's going on here?" I asked, knowing the likelihood of getting a straight answer was quite low.

Everyone just smirked at my ignorance and kept working away at their projects.

"I know that you are excited to see your bride, Mr. Ludy," said Feminine Grace, joining me in my stroll toward the small mountain cottage. "But I hope you will understand that she will not be joining us just yet."

"Uh . . . OK," I said, mystified and not at all mentally adroit enough to deal with the concept of Leslie not "joining us yet."

"What is this place?" I asked Feminine Grace as we approached the front porch where Mr. Purity was busy sweeping and setting everything in perfect order.

"It will be obvious soon enough," she said with a warm smile.

I walked up the steps to the cozy cottage and admired the handiwork of Mr. Purity. "You won't find a speck of dirt in the whole place!" he said with an affable grin. "I've been getting this place ready for the past twelve weeks."

I decided to play along. But that didn't keep the countless unanswered questions from knocking around within my mind. *Mr. Smith? A mountain cottage in the middle of nowhere? Twelve weeks of preparation? What is all this?*

As I entered the small abode, I was greeted with a bounty of rose petals strewn upon the floor. It appeared that Sacred had already been here. There was a roaring fire crackling in the living area just ahead, causing a blanket of romantic warmth to swarm me in its embrace as I stepped over the enchanting threshold.

Soft, classical music was emanating from the wood-paneled walls, stirring an oh-so-subtle hint of symphonic romance into the air.

"Mr. Ludy, you've got your wish," Mr. Purity said. "You've earned yourself an interview with Mr. Smith."

"Who is Mr. Smith?" I asked softly, truly perplexed.

"You've won yourself a fifth interview, my friend. Enjoy it!" With that he smiled grandly and closed the front door to the cottage leaving me all alone.

I stood there for a second in the foyer, attempting to wrap my mind around the events currently circling about me. I had waited seven weeks for another blue sticky note from the League. This morning when I found one resting on my pillow, I never would have guessed that it would have led to this . . . this, whatever it was, now unfolding before me.

I hesitantly stepped into this charming chalet. Candles were burning all around the small living room, with flames swaying in perfect rhythm with the oboe solo currently whispering its emotive song in the background.

"Hello?" I called uncomfortably. "Mr. Smith?"

There was no answer. I peered into the small kitchen area. There sat a large ceramic mug filled with hot chai tea, steaming happily on the marble countertop. A blue sticky note that was attached to it read, *Make yourself comfortable, Peeps!*

I picked up the mug and carried it into the living room, finding myself a place to sit by the fire in an elegant leather wingback chair. Whether or not an interview with Mr. Smith would be worth all this to-do was still to be determined, but in the meantime, I was loving this.

I sat in the tall chair, sipping at my chai and staring about the room. On a small end table near my right elbow I noticed a dusty leather-bound book. I picked it up and read the spine: *With Fire and Sword.* It was another one of my favorites. I smiled as I opened the front cover. There, inside the front cover of the book was a blue sticky note that read: *I see why you like it so much!*

But what was strange is that the note was obviously in Mr. Purity's handwriting, but the name he signed was *Mr. Smith.*

That's odd, I thought to myself, setting the book back down. In fact this whole escapade was quite odd. *Who was this Mr. Smith, anyway? Was Mr. Smith some kind of third-party arbitration judge used for highly sensitive matters of heavenly importance? Was he human? Angelic? And where was he anyway?*

As the minutes passed, I pulled out the love letter Leslie had written me and read it afresh, relishing every word. Boy, did I want to kiss her!

After I had once again tucked away her letter, I looked up and was surprised to see a painter's easel set up only a few feet from where I was sitting. A fresh piece of fine drawing paper was taped onto its front. I glanced beside the easel and, sure enough, there was a handful of sketching pencils, an eraser, and, of course, a blue sticky note sitting underneath another fresh mug full of chai. The note read: *Peeps, thought you might wish to sketch while you wait.*

I shook my head with disbelieving astonishment. When I was younger, I had enjoyed pencil drawing, but over time the skill had fallen into disrepair. Until these past forty-nine days, that is. I now was fully realizing that it was Sacred who must have inspired the idea to have me pick up sketching once again. I had begun, over the past few weeks, to make "love sketches" for Leslie. They weren't very professional looking;

in fact, most of them were downright awful. But they seemed to bring Leslie to life. In fact, they brought tears to her eyes. And whereas she might giggle at my dog that looked far more akin to a hump-backed horse, she would turn to me and with warmth in her voice whisper, "It's perfect, Beef!"

I shook my head in disbelief as I picked up a pencil and pulled the easel a bit closer. I felt like I was twenty-two again, wooing the heart of my beloved. I placed the tip of my pencil against the paper and paused, wondering, *What should I draw?* Soon an idea flowed into my mind and then out the tip of my pencil. As the minutes passed, I was smiling to myself. How many people in the world get to go to work and do this?

I used that eraser as if it were salt on a bland stew, but after about twenty minutes a likeness began to come into view. As I scribbled away on that piece of drawing paper, a story began to unfold and, in a strange way, it began to teach me as I drew.

There were two figures in my picture. My original idea was to draw me standing with a sword, my left foot placed authoritatively on the neck of a wild beast, with Leslie clinging to my side, gazing up at me with one of those "Oh, Eric, you're my hero!" kind of looks. Yes, it was a sappy and overly romantic idea, but it's precisely those sorts of overly romanticized pictures that Leslie loves. I even had a title for my picture: "Edwin and His Fair Maiden." But as I started tracing the outer edge of "me" on the paper, something nudged me to make my hair look like Mr. Marvelous's and to give myself a squarer jaw. I even added a streak of silver into the darkened wavy locks. Then instead of drawing my scrawny body, I shaped my body into the hulking replica of Mr. Purity. And for a little splash of humor, I erased the sword and put a kitchen broom in his hand.

As I began to draw the "Leslie" portion of the picture, I found myself drawing a rather beautiful collaboration between the forms and faces of Sacred and Feminine Grace. In a sense, it was Leslie, but it seemed to symbolize even more than Leslie.

I sat back and viewed my picture, attempting to get a broader perspective. And while I nibbled at my lower lip and squinted my right eye, another idea came to me. I vigorously erased the wild beast subjected to humiliation beneath the heel of my left boot and, in its place, began to sketch Jimmy the Shrimp in all his inglorious ugliness. I must admit, drawing Jimmy the Shrimp as a helpless defeated foe was supremely pleasurable.

Now in all fairness, this picture with all my description here sounds a bit grander than it actually looks in real life. But all in all, I would say for a fifth-grade-level artist, like myself, this could be considered my magnum opus.

It took me approximately fifty-four minutes to finish my masterpiece. And it was as I brushed off the final flecks of eraser dust that I began to realize what I had just drawn.

I know this is going to sound bizarre. But I had somehow inadvertently drawn the essence of Great Sex. There it was staring back at me in all its mysterious brilliance.

I picked up the pencil one more time and added nail wounds to the warrior's hands and then set my pencil down. It was brilliant.

"It's perfect!" said a female voice from just behind my shoulder.

The voice startled me. And I turned around to see Sacred smiling.

"Have you figured out the mystery yet, Peeps?" she said with a twinkle in her eyes.

"I don't think so," I said, "but I sense I'm getting close."

"Have you met Mr. Smith yet?" asked Mr. Purity, who was standing on the far edge of the small living room, on the other side of my easel, flanked by Mr. Marvelous and Feminine Grace.

"No, not yet," I said, disappointed. "He never showed up."

"Oh, he showed up," affirmed Mr. Purity.

I was perplexed. Did Mr. Smith slip in unnoticed while I was drawing?

"Peeps," Sacred interrupted my thoughts. "You've been thinking from the start that Great Sex was an actual personality with a set of quirky behaviors, a British accent, and a propensity to wax eloquent and rhyme. How did you put it in your first chapter? 'Great Sex,' you said, 'is William Wallace meets Lord Alfred Tennyson,' or something like that."

"He's not?"

"Don't get me wrong," Sacred said with a wry grin. "He is all that. But he's not exactly what you are thinking he is. You are right that he's real, and you've got him pegged, but you're just a little mixed up in your terminology."

I wasn't quite following what Sacred was saying.

"Great Sex is apricot and walnut varenikis," said Mr. Purity as if everything was quite obvious to him.

"Excuse me?" I said, not quite understanding why a fruit-and-nut concoction had just been tied with Great Sex.

"What?" roared Purity with shock. "You have never tried an apricot and walnut varenikis?"

"I'm afraid not." I confessed.

"You really are a beginner!" He laughed. "Oh, it's the tastiest, most dignified dessert this side of the Ukraine—chewy noodle dumplings stuffed with dried apricots and walnuts, then sprinkled with a cinnamon-crumb topping. It's heaven come to earth!"

"And Great Sex is somehow similar?" I added, a bit confused.

"They are one in the same!" He spouted confidently. "They are both merely the scrumptious result of certain quality ingredients, prepared a certain way, and cooked for a certain amount of time."

"Are you saying that Great Sex is not a person?" I asked with a bit of consternation. After all, my entire book was based on my finally interviewing this guy.

"Would you call chewy noodle dumplings stuffed with dried apricots and walnuts, then sprinkled with a cinnamon-crumb topping, a person, Mr. Ludy?"

"Well, then, who is Mr. Smith?"

"You're talking with him," answered Mr. Purity.

"*You* are Mr. Smith?"

"We all are," interjected Sacred softly. "We are the certain quality ingredients that not only know how to prepare your life to perfection but also how to cook your life and bring out the most perfect aroma and taste."

"So Mr. Smith is Great Sex?"

"That's correct," answered Mr. Purity.

"And you all are Mr. Smith?"

"That too is correct."

"So this whole time I have been pining away for an opportunity to interview Great Sex and . . ."

"Again, you are correct."

I sat in stunned silence. What was my publisher going to say? I had promised them an interview with Great Sex, and yet Great

Sex can't talk because he is a chewy noodle dumpling stuffed with dried apricots and walnuts?!

"Peeps," Sacred said warmly, "you do realize that you are currently in the room with the foremost experts on Great Sex? And that technically by interviewing us you are, in a manner of speaking, interviewing Great Sex?"

I pondered that for a moment. Then my eyes turned and once again perused my pencil drawing. It was a picture of the League doing what they do best—bringing victory, closeness, love, and beauty. The League was Great Sex!

"You all are truly amazing," I confessed as I allowed the depth of this newfound reality to sink into my understanding.

The four members of the illustrious League found themselves a place to sit and we embarked upon the fifth and final interview—the interview with Great Sex, or should I say, the interview with Mr. Smith.

In the following chapter, I have attempted to capture the extraordinary events that followed.

CHAPTER 17

Great Sex

When you gaze into the beautiful, majestic faces of glory, it demands something more than mere everyday language to articulate its grandeur. The awe-inspiring beauty of Purity, Holiness, True Masculinity, and True Femininity is stunning, poetic, divine, elegant, muscular, fragile, fragrant, vulnerable, strong yet shockingly soft.

These four noble heroes gathered together in one room is enough to take your breath away and leave you basking in the glory of the Almighty.

When God penned the Song of Solomon, He enunciated with canonized eloquence the force and the holiness of sexuality. But He didn't describe this divine picture of sexual intimacy using "everyday" language. He used poetry and song. To God, sex is not a mundane, common thing, but rather an extraordinary, set-apart experience, deserving the highest, most beautiful language to describe it, for it is a holy giving, a holy sharing. It is mystical and divine, and I, Eric Ludy, was preparing to actually interview it.

I pulled out my notepad and pen and repositioned myself for this all-important interview. I looked about the candlelit room. It was striking, and the personalities seated around me were even more stunning than the room itself. I was in awe. I noticed that my right knee had begun to knock. I placed my hand upon my jiggling knee in an attempt to settle it.

"Mr. Ludy," said Mr. Marvelous, "I would encourage you never to lose that boyish sense of wonder and awe. A great man never trembles before the enemy, but he always trembles before God."

"Do you remember your wedding night?" said Feminine Grace sweetly.

"Of course I do," I answered.

"Do you remember how your knee shook the same way that night?"

She was right. It had. It was the same holy anticipation that was coursing through my body. It was an expectancy of something heavenly, something choreographed by God Himself.

"Mr. Ludy," Mr. Purity added, "we will allow you to ask your questions in a moment, but first I feel it is imperative to remind you of a couple of things before we begin."

I nodded.

"First, our work is not merely about Great Sex. Great Sex, in fact, is merely a delectable fruit born as a result of our even deeper work within the soul."

"We are commissioned by God," interjected Sacred, "to first and foremost author a divine romance between Jesus Christ and humanity."

"Precisely," nodded Mr. Purity. "We are the hands and feet of the gospel in a believer's life. Jesus has given His people life. And it is our job to bring that 'life' out of the realm of theory and into the realm of reality. Each of us makes the work that Jesus Christ accomplished thousands of years ago actually *work* in the human life today."

"When you allowed Mr. Purity to work on you for the first time over seventeen years ago," Sacred said, "the 'life' of Jesus began to grow within your body and the Almighty commissioned me to enter your being in order to make that happen."

"And as you allowed Sacred to take possession of your life," said Mr. Marvelous, "it freed me to begin to shape you into a man. For a man is nothing more than the perfect work of Purity and Holiness upon the clay of yielded masculinity."

"And that is where I come in," said Feminine Grace with a smile, "for it was when you gave Mr. Marvelous a voice in your life that he gave you eyes to appreciate and protect me."

"You see, Mr. Ludy," said Mr. Purity, "the process that you embarked upon over seventeen years ago with Jesus is the same process that brings you closer to Leslie even now. The reason we do all our purifying, consecrating, man-making, woman-valuing work inside of you is to bring about a clear picture of Jesus Christ in this world. It's so that Christ might be seen without you standing in the way obscuring the view."

"And the very mechanics that have made for a great love story between you and Jesus Christ," said Feminine Grace warmly, "are the very same mechanics that have served to make your love story with Leslie so divine."

"Great Sex, Peeps," interjected Sacred, "is the result of the same recipe used to cook up Great Intimacy with Jesus Christ. We, the League, do our work in order that lovers, both heavenly and earthly, might be drawn closer and closer together."

"So our first point, Mr. Ludy," said Purity, "is that we, the League, do what we do for the fame of Jesus Christ and not for the fame of Great Sex!" He paused and then continued, "However, due to the massive attack being waged against human sexuality today, we each felt that your efforts to bring back the truth in this arena of sex might be important to support."

"We have taken you through this seeming obstacle course of refinement," smirked Sacred, "because we had to make sure you remembered that Great Sex is only an outflow of Jesus Christ crowned King and ruling with love within the human soul."

"You really caused a fuss among the League when you requested an interview with Great Sex," smiled Mr. Marvelous.

"You should have seen Mr. Purity!" laughed Feminine Grace, "He nearly burst a blood vessel!"

"I read your first two chapters," smiled Purity, "and then began to settle down a bit. But when I first heard the notion that Eric and Leslie Ludy were going to write a book on Great Sex, I wanted to smack you so hard upside the head that you'd forget which end was up and hopefully forgo the whole convoluted notion."

"You can thank me," said Mr. Marvelous. "I stood up for you and told this big oaf over here that I believed you could handle the necessary purging in order to be prepared to write on such a sacred topic."

"Thanks," I said, not quite knowing if I meant it.

"And you didn't let me down," he said warmly.

"The second point we wish to make before we begin," said Mr. Purity, "is in regards to a serious misconception about what Great Sex is."

"Great Sex," said Mr. Marvelous, "is not a mere physical act."

"That's right, Mr. Ludy," added Feminine Grace. "And this is a very important point to understand. For just like that apricot and walnut varenikis we referred to before, Great Sex is a process of preparation, waiting, *and then* enjoyment."

"If you fail to see, Mr. Ludy," said Mr. Marvelous, "that Great Sex involves the sacred waiting for God's perfect timing, the honoring of holy marriage covenant, the wooing of a heart throughout the day, the single-eye of adoration for your spouse alone, the tender thoughtful reminders of affection, and the constant attitude and princely demeanor of Christ unto your bride —then it would be like forgetting to clean and slice the apricots, forgoing the preparation of the chewy noodle dumplings, avoiding the mixing of the luscious filling, then sticking an empty pan in the oven at 450 degrees, and discovering that after twenty minutes there is merely a burnt dessert pan and nothing magical inside it."

"Great Sex is a result of living out Jesus Christ and loving Him, as well as your spouse, with every word, attitude, and action."

"When Purity has his way, Holiness has her sway, Manhood is maturing, and Femininity is growing, then Great Sex has already been discovered. Now it is just a matter of finding it better and better every day of married life."

They went on like this for another hour. Back and forth they talked, finishing each other's sentences, fully understanding and in agreement with each other's opinions and thoughts. It was perfect. It all made sense. These were the ingredients that made sex actually work. These past twelve weeks, had been for me, a picture of the sexual process. The League had walked me through the art of sacred foreplay—the preparation of a pure heart and body, the sacred waiting of the trusting soul, accompanied by the heart-stirring anticipation of the end product. They had brought me to this destination, this cottage, to give me a real-life picture of what takes place within the heart, body, and life of a sexual being yielded to God's lead.

"Why did you call yourselves Mr. Smith?" I asked later in the conversation.

Mr. Purity laughed and said, "Well, we had to come up with a name that fit the four of us. Mr. Marvelous proposed it, and I thought it sounded perfect—it's understated and yet still quite dignified."

"I thought it lent a very mysterious and rather romantic panache to the entire experience," answered Sacred. "After all, with a name like Mr. Smith, you must be hiding something."

"We love to leave a bit of romantic mystery in the air," answered Feminine Grace, "causing people to wonder how this drama will all play out. You were convinced that Great Sex was a person in his own right, separate from the League. So we gave you a name and set your imagination running wild."

"If we had told you, in the very beginning, that Great Sex was the League," added Sacred, "then the process would have been too predictable. Finding Great Sex, my friend, just like finding the God who created it, is anything but common and predictable. You never know if it will be a sprig of lilac, a bunch of daisies, a cluster of henna blooms, a bouquet of lilies, or a single daffodil. If it were a room carpeted in rose petals that awaited you, wouldn't it be more enchanting to have it sneak up on you and surprise you?"

"Great Sex is amazing and unpredictable," added Mr. Marvelous, "and therefore, we couldn't bring you on a journey in which you would know the ending. Wouldn't that have defeated the purpose entirely?"

I don't know if I actually said more than four words in the entire time that remained. I mean, what was there to say? What could I really add that would make the conversation better? I just loved listening to them talk. They loved what they did. They made people happy for a living. They brought the freedom, the peace, and the blissful joy of Christ to everyone with whom they worked.

◻ ◻ ◻

Mr. Purity.

To most of the living, breathing world he is nothing more than a skinny nerd in high-water pants and suspenders. But in reality, he is the introductory ingredient into the most breathtaking beauties of Great Sex. He is the bodyguard of the soul, kicking out the junk and keeping safe the jewels. His method seems a bit harsh to some. He brings conviction. But to those who have fallen in love with Jesus Christ and are longing for more and more of Him, conviction is the light shining on everything that still stands in the way of such awe-inspiring intimacy with our heavenly King.

Everyone wants Great Sex. But only those who are intimately familiar with the work of Mr. Purity, and the application of his muscular force upon the garbage within our souls, are privileged to ever meet Mr. Smith.

□ □ □

Sacred.

To most people on planet earth, she is a frumpy goody-two-shoes with frizzy hair and a high-and-mighty attitude. But in reality, she is the romance and love of heaven come down to earth. She is radiant. She is the Spirit of God unto Holiness. She separates God's people from their Flesh in order that they might fully enjoy the blessings of God's kingdom riches. And if one allows, Sacred will choreograph and lead a life into the arms of exquisite beauty, extraordinary joy, and blissful closeness with both Jesus Christ and an earthly spouse.

Sacred asks for our entire life. Everything must come under her sacred keeping. And then she will ask us to wait while she works her painful and yet beautiful magic in our soul. She asks us to trust that in God's perfect timing she will remove the sweet smelling product of her labors from out of the heavenly oven, hand us a fork, and say, "Enjoy!"

Everyone wants Great Sex. But it simply cannot be found unless Sacred first grooms the heart, the mind, and the body to fully appreciate it.

□ □ □

Mr. Marvelous.

For most people, the idea of the existence of Mr. Marvelous is simply preposterous. To believe in True Masculinity is akin to believing in the tooth fairy or the abominable snowman. But whether one chooses to believe in his existence doesn't change the fact that Mr. Marvelous is very real, and his noble presence is an extremely important component to Great Sex.

A great man knows how to love a woman well. He knows how to move at the pace of a woman's heart and study a woman's deepest needs. He knows how to woo a woman and never pressure her. He knows how to inspire a woman and protect a woman's virtue. A great man knows how to take his spiritual wallet full of Purity and Holiness, and exchange it into the practical currency of being a Christ-built husband and father. A great man inspires a woman to be a great woman. He is an initiator in love, but he will never initiate outside the bounds of Mr. Purity's and Sacred's governance. He is the leader in a relationship with his girl. He must press her toward Christ, love her into the arms of Purity and Sacred's keeping, and inspire her to allow Feminine Grace to build and shape her femininity.

Everyone wants Great Sex. But Great Sex is inaccessible to the man unwilling to rise to the superlative heights of masculine glory and be forged by the fire of God into a heroic picture of Christ's love and grace. All a man must do is step in this noble direction and Great Sex opens up like a frontier before him, waiting to be discovered more and more for the rest of his manly journey on earth.

□ □ □

Feminine Grace.

Like her masculine counterpart, Feminine Grace is considered a farce, a joke, a puritanical idea of yesteryear once peddled by the overly prude, chastity-belted virgins of a bygone era. In fact, ironically, the idea sounds unromantic to most young women of today, for it smacks of shapeless dresses, dreary countenances, frizzy hair, and doleful silence. Yet in fact true femininity is exquisite beauty, a radiant joyful glow, a smile that can thaw the most frozen hearts, a poetic dignity, an enchanting softness, a blissful elegance, and a regal decorum that far surpasses that of a royal court. True Femininity will cause a king to rise, a prince to bow, and a knight to stutter with breathless awe.

Feminine Grace inspires a man to be a great man. She is a responder in love, always patient and prayerful, allowing the man to take the lead. She is an artist with encouragement and praise, building muscles into the framework of a masculine soul with her words of respect and honor. She is in her marriage, as the believer is unto Christ. She is given to her man, wholly, fully, and without reticence. She is adoring and attentive to his every movement of spirit, longing to see him encounter Jesus in a fuller, more intimate way. She innately knows how to arrive at the small mountain cottage snuggled warmly amidst the cloak of evergreens. God has given her the map to the treasure of Great Sex. And as a great man studies her heart, she can help him reach this majestic and beautiful destination.

▫ ▫ ▫

These four personalities, when working in harmony, are a wonder to behold. They lead one into the holy of holies with Jesus Christ—and they lead a married couple into the holy of holies of intimate love and givenness.

□ □ □

I was sitting in that leather wingback chair pondering these things. The room was silent but for the crackle of the fire and a soft saxophone melody in the background. I was transfixed by the shadows of candle flames dancing throughout the room. I was happy—immeasurably happy.

Only minutes earlier, Sacred had said, "Peeps, we have one more surprise for you. Sit right here and don't go anywhere. It will only be a couple more minutes."

The fifth interview had proved quite amazing. Everything about it was divine, as if heaven had come to earth and parked itself in the middle of my soul. I was a man in love. And this wasn't just your store-bought variety of love; this was a special import straight from heaven's storehouse. I was whispering to Jesus as I waited. I love my God so desperately it hurts. He has given me so much, and I don't deserve any of it. And for some reason, He entrusted a girl named Leslie to me, to love and cherish.

At five o'clock that very morning I had kissed her on the lips in order to wake her up. If I had known that all this would transpire in my life today and that I would have to wait until this late in the day to see her again, I would have planted a princely kiss on her and maybe remained stuck to her pretty face all morning.

I wanted to kiss my bride. It was that simple.

Suddenly there was a knock on the front door of the cottage.

My heart was filled with anticipation and romantic longing. I stood to my feet, my right knee knocking, and ambled carefully to the door, trying not to crush any of the rose petals that lay artistically upon the tiled floor.

I reached the front door and opened it, wholly expecting to see the radiant beauty of my bride. But there was no one there.

I looked down at my feet and saw near the threshold of the door a cluster of lilies, the very same bouquet I had purchased for Leslie earlier that afternoon. I stooped down and picked them up and realized, as I did, that underneath the flowery sprigs were the love letters I had written to Leslie that morning. I smiled, looking around for Sacred, knowing that this was her fine work.

I turned and reentered the small mountain abode, closing the door behind me. As I entered the small living area, I was surprised to see the face of an angel. I've actually never seen an angel, so I'm not sure if this is what an angel looks like, but "angel" is the most beautiful, strong, yet delicate word I can think to describe such a picture. It was Leslie. She was elegant, royal, mysterious, and seemed to squeeze Sacred's invisible hand as if drawing some unseen power out of her dear attendant's embrace.

She seemed just as shocked as I was.

"Beef!" she whispered.

I struggled to speak, but I didn't struggle to move. I crossed the room quashing every last rose petal that stood in my way, hoping that they might move my feet more quickly in the direction of my bride. I pressed the lilies into her open hand and laid a princely kiss upon her lips, the sort of which Mr. Marvelous would have been proud. When I set her down after twirling her about, I ran my hand tenderly through her dark brown locks and whispered, "You are truly lovely, Leslie! Truly lovely!"

And there in the distance, near the back door of the small cottage, through which Leslie must have entered, I spied four smiling faces hidden in the shadows. They waved. Mr. Marvelous gave me a thumbs-up, and I could hear Sacred squeal with delight.

◻ ◻ ◻

This was supposed to be a book to expose Imposter Sex and introduce Great Sex. But it turned out to be a book about finding the muscle of Purity, the romance of Holiness, the nobility of Manhood, and the grace of Femininity. "What a strange development," you might say. However, I'd like to think this strange development will ultimately prove far more helpful to you than a quick interview with Great Sex ever would. For now you have in your possession the secret directions to finding this long-lost buried treasure.

What should you do if you hold in your possession a map to buried treasure, or as four of my good friends might say, "the recipe for the ultimate apricot and walnut varenikis"? My advice would be, dare not ever lose it!

Part 2

Leslie

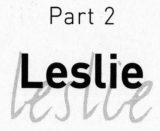

CHAPTER 18

It's All True!

My sweet husband is what you would call a *romanticist*. A romanticist, by definition, is one who strongly believes that life is romantic in its very nature if you have an eye to see it. But romance for Eric isn't merely soft candle glow and Wordsworth; it's seeing the magical edge in every mundane moment of life. And as a result, he is rarely in a bad mood. He loves life so much that he actually complains about an odd pain inside his stomach from so much happiness. I've offered to give him some vitamins for his "odd pain," but he animatedly refuses, not wishing to mess with success.

Great Sex is not a myth in our marriage. It is merely a matter of fact. We enjoy our marriage far more than we probably should. We laugh, hug, kiss, cuddle, squeeze, pinch, caress, and whisper sweet nothings as if Windsor, Colorado, were about to be destroyed by a nuclear warhead and we'd better make the most of the time we have left.

Marriage for Eric and me isn't a duty but an absolute delight. We honestly *love* loving each other. We spend our days thinking about how privileged we are to be living out a real-life fairy tale. Loving one person for a lifetime is easy if you love that person well.

So combine the fact that Eric is a romanticist with the fact that he is in a supremely romantic marriage and you get the first seventeen chapters of this book. As much as my husband loves what he and I share in our marriage, it bothers him that so few others actually even realize that what we have isn't supposed to be unusual. He wants everyone to taste the sacred delicacies of holy sexuality.

Now I will admit that Eric has quite an imagination. I, for one, love him for it. But I realize that there are those of you out there who may get a little uncomfortable around the "romantic" breed and that it would be easy for you to write off the previous seventeen chapters as fanciful allegory. But I wish to let you know that everything you just read was real. It all happened *almost* exactly as he said. I will admit, it was a very imaginative rendition of reality, but it was reality nonetheless.

As I said, my husband has a knack for taking the mundane and making it magical. You may, for instance, prefer to view Purity as merely a concept, but Eric battles for these concepts every day of his life, and I think I agree with him that these ideas actually have personality; they have a manner, a method, a voice. And if anyone would be equipped to bring out the true personification of these illustrious heroes, it would be my husband.

Eric has the uncanny ability to bring romance to the otherwise stale dimensions of life. The other day, for instance, he initiated a conversation with me on how we can make getting ready in the morning more fun and exciting.

"I want to wake up every day to an enchanted life," he said to me while shaving this past Thursday. "Imagine getting out of bed in the morning," he continued enthusiastically, "and actually looking forward to the process of getting ready!"

Eric simply refuses to allow life to be uninteresting and humdrum. He does this with our lives and our love story every day. And so, it is no surprise to me that he took what nearly everyone else on planet earth would have deemed merely twelve ordinary weeks, and he allowed them to become something truly enchanting and unforgettable. On the surface they were twelve supremely challenging weeks, full of deep conviction, challenge, sickness, frigid cold, and the emotional trauma of losing an unborn child; but underneath all the ice, the two of us discovered twelve weeks of profound joy, beautiful intimacy, exquisite romance, and the greatest sex.

When you are married, every day can be a day for Great Sex. But it all depends on whether you approach that day as a romanticist or as a dreariologist. (Dreariologists, by the way, are the opposite of romanticists. They expect to find misery in each day and they inevitably do.) Just like there is an imposter version of sex, there is an imposter version of life. Eric may be a little overly sentimental and romantically effusive for your taste, but if you take what he has to say you will realize that he is giving you more than just the recipe for Great Sex; he's sharing the recipe for Great Life.

When he leaves the house for Cup of Loodles Café, I just smile, knowing that he's gone off to fight battles for his princess. He comes back with stories to tell of villains he's vanquished, heroes he's set free, and then out from behind his back he reveals a handful of lilies he plucked from the meadows just outside the king's castle.

Every man should be a romanticist. And I may be a bit biased, but I think every man should be just like my Beef. Give my husband a large ceramic mug filled with chai tea and let the adventure begin. Don't let him fool you. He's not a mediocre man. He's a marvelous man, and he loves me in a marvelous way.

◻ ◻ ◻

Let me catch you up on a few details you may be still wondering about in regard to the first seventeen chapters of this book.

First of all, we did get this manuscript turned in on time. I know many of you were a bit concerned about this matter when Eric announced that he had spent forty-nine days loving me rather than attending to this book. But Sacred was correct. If you want to write a book on Great Sex, then it makes sense that you spend a lot of time in the laboratory.

Second, for all you who are interested in the further adventures of Deuce Johnson, which by the way is not his real name, I'm happy to announce that he is thriving in the kingdom of God. Eric arrived back from Loodles the other day and told me that he saw Deuce meeting with Mr. Purity near the back of the café. So the news is "onward and upward!"

Third, we are still not sure how my love letter made it from the Coffee Grounds in north Fort Collins all the way to our kitchen counter in Windsor, but the two of us are placing our bets on the fact that it was Feminine Grace. Leave it to a woman to pull off a romantic stunt of such massive proportions!

Fourth, Eric and I are thrilled to announce that we have officially moved beyond the beginner's level as a result of the writing of this book. And I must forewarn any and all of you married couples who would dare to follow in our footsteps—such exquisite pleasure is not for those of faint heart and weak constitution.

Fifth, like many of you, I grew concerned with Eric's galloneous intake of chai tea during the formation of this book. Not only was he visiting the little boy's room with stunning regularity, but I feared the caffeine was a bit overcomplementary to his already energetic personality. So fear not, all you health-savvy readers; I have initiated a two-mug-per-week rule that went into effect just this last Monday.

And finally, for all of you unmarried readers out there who have specific questions regarding *meeting Mr. Smith* for yourself someday, I am pleased to announce that I am here to help. This second section of the book is my opportunity to do what I do best—make truth practical, usable, and effective. I'm going to be answering the dooziest of all the doozy questions in the upcoming pages.

Just as Great Sex demands the participation of a man and a woman, so this book needs a little feminine touch added to all Eric's adorable snips and snails and puppy dog tails. Now I realize that there may be a few questions that I miss in my attempt to cover all these questions, but it is my hope that the biggest, juiciest, and most confusing questions will be addressed for you in this forthcoming section. And please check out www.setapartlife.com/mistersmith for some bonus questions and answers that were not included in this book.

Where Eric is a romanticist, I am a romanticizer, which for

those of you who might not know, is an organizer with a romantic propensity. I love getting things done, but I love getting them done with style if at all possible. Eric leans more toward eloquence, whereas I lean more towards clarity and conciseness. So where my portion of this book may not rivet you to your seat with a mesmerizing storyline, it will get your questions answered quickly, effectively, and with a hint of romantic spice thrown in. Such is my job as the romanticizer in our marriage and on this project.

Oh, and two more bits of information before we jump in and begin to solve all the world's problems:

Eric and I love the poetry and majesty of language and therefore felt it most appropriate to use the King James Version of the Bible (KJV) when quoting Scripture in this book. It's the romantic and noble version of the Bible. Though the King James Version can often be a bit troublesome and weighty, Eric and I love it for its grandeur and higher language. There are a couple of exceptions in the upcoming pages where you will find that we used a different translation, but we attempted to use the King James Version as much as possible.

And finally, please remember that Jimmy the Shrimp (the Flesh) is not a fan of this book. He hated Eric's section, and he's not going to like mine much either. You should expect a few uncomfortable moments internally as you read the following pages. But please don't buy the Shrimp's sales pitch that God's ways are miserable and crusty. It's simply not true. If you take Mr. Purity, Sacred, Mr. Marvelous, and Feminine Grace seriously, then you will soon be discovering that the words "Wow!" and "Whoa!" are far too weak to describe what is happening in your heart and life.

CHAPTER 19

What About . . . ?

Candid Q & A About Sex, Lust, Purity, and More

QUESTION: What does God really think about premarital sex?

Last week I read an e-mail from a spunky young bride-to-be named Cassie. She wanted to know, "If Mike and I really love each other, and we've already made a lifelong commitment to each other, what is the difference between having sex now and waiting until we are married?" This is a common question among young Christians today. Why do wedding vows make such a difference to God when it comes to the timing of sex? What's really so wrong with expressing your love to someone physically before marriage, especially if you are planning to spend your lives together anyway?

As I pondered Cassie's e-mail, I (Leslie) remember asking similar questions not too many years ago. Growing up in church, I'd heard vague explanations of this seemingly overly strict Christian rule, and none of them really satisfied me. "Sex is so much better when you save it until marriage," a guest speaker at my girls' study group once told us. "It's like Christmas morning—the presents lose their luster if you open them ahead of time!"

I have since learned that there was a lot of truth in what that speaker said. But because no one ever had told me *why* sex was so much better if you waited for marriage, it seemed like a weak argument. Then there was the much-overused line from our youth pastor: "Why eat a greasy hamburger now when you could have a steak dinner later?" That one never really moved me, because I like hamburgers far better than steak. And besides, the hamburger analogy, like the Christmas present one, didn't explain the reason *why* sex in marriage was supposedly superior to sex right now.

"Sex before marriage is a sin!" bellowed a passionate pastor at a convention I attended one summer. Even though I didn't appreciate the manner in which the man delivered the statement, I was impressed by his forthrightness. I went home that night and tried to find "premarital sex" in the Bible, wanting to see for myself that it was indeed, touted as a sin. But all I could find were mentions of something vague called "sexual immorality," which as far as I knew could mean adultery, homosexuality, or any number of other acts that didn't relate to premarital sex. Was having sex before marriage really a big deal to God?

Common sense, the advice of my parents and leaders, and scare tactics used by school counselors and youth pastors convinced me that sleeping around with multiple partners was certainly not a smart idea, as it often created a number of serious problems such as unwanted pregnancy, sexually transmitted diseases, and, at least for a woman, emotional scarring from feelings of being used. But what about when two people really loved each other? What if they planned to spend their lives together? What was so important about one trip down the aisle? Couldn't you just say some wedding vows in your heart and be covered?

It wasn't until God began to truly invade this part of my life and teach me the wonder of His ways that I began to understand this area more clearly. In my own life and love story, I experienced the amazing beauty of following God's ways and reaping the incredible benefits. I personally discovered that my small group speaker was right: sex in marriage *is* far superior when you wait. In fact Great Sex only shows up when you experience intimacy in God's context—marriage. Anything outside of that will be nothing but a cheap counterfeit of the real thing . . . Imposter Sex in all his debased, lackluster glory.

But how could I explain that to Cassie in a way she would truly understand? Just writing her back and saying, "Trust me, saving sex till marriage is the way to go," seemed like a cop-out. Cassie, and so many others like her, wanted more than a pat answer.

So I decided to put the answer in terms of the story Eric told in the first part of this book.

Most people think that the source of this dilemma is Mr. Purity—so they're a bit surprised to know that Purity is not actually the one responsible for the saving-sex-until marriage edict. Saving sex until marriage was, in fact, Sacred's idea. Purity merely gives people the ability to carry out her prescription.

As I think back over my love story with Eric, I can say with confidence that Eric and I found Great Sex in our marriage. We found something beautiful, blissful, and utterly beyond any version of sex the world had ever presented to us. And though Purity was instrumental in helping us with this discovery, it was Sacred who ultimately presented us with the prize. Though at the time I wasn't aware of Sacred's presence in my love story with Eric, it was Sacred's work that made our love story stand out so dramatically from other guy/girl relationships. Eric and I grew up in a secular culture that had turned the concept of sex into a selfish, animalistic, and debased act. The Christian world we were part of typically treated sex as something dangerous that needed to be harnessed and regulated—therefore the Christian version of sex seemed stiff, legalistic, and depressing. We desperately needed God's perspective. And that's where Sacred came in. As she subtly unveiled the pattern that leads to Great Sex, it was the first time I understood the *why* behind saving sex until marriage. As we prayed, talked, and searched the Scriptures, there were two important truths that Sacred revealed to us.

1. *Great Sex, in its very essence, is sacred.* Imposter Sex, as evidenced every day in our culture, is aggressive, obnoxious, and very much in-your-face. But Great Sex, by its very nature, is private, hidden, mysterious, and even secretive—as demonstrated earlier in this book. That is because God designed sex to be supremely intimate—and intimacy can only flourish through privacy, sanctuary, and trust. One of the primary reasons Eric and I enjoy such blissful intimacy in our relationship is that we keep sacred things sacred. We don't share details about our intimate relationship with the world. We have designed our bedroom as a sanctuary—a set-apart place for just the two of us to enjoy our love. And we don't allow the raucous, careless attitudes of culture to creep into our romance—

we keep television, newspapers, and the stresses of life *out* of our private time together (and as much as possible, out of the rest of daily life as well!)

Our culture's version of sex is casual and debased. But God designed sex to be holy. The Song of Solomon demonstrates this beautifully. When God talks about sex, He doesn't describe intimate love between a man and a woman in a matter-of-fact, casual way. Rather, He chooses the highest form of language—poetry. He is a God of romance and beauty. He delights in His children discovering the wonder of pure, undefiled love. The Song of Solomon, in the Jewish understanding, has been compared to "the holy of holies" in the Jewish temple. The holy of holies was not a place to be entered into lightly. Only once a year, after the high priest had carefully examined himself for sin and offered sacrifices, would he enter the holiest place of the temple to stand before God—with much fear and trembling. He had a rope tied around his ankle that trailed behind him, in case he was struck dead in God's presence and the others had to drag his body out.

It was believed by many Jews that if this priest had even the slightest trace of sin in his heart upon entering the holiest place of all, not only would he be struck dead in the presence of God, but the whole earth would be destroyed as a result.

In other words, the holy of holies was a big deal. It wasn't something to be haphazard about. It was a place to enter cautiously, only after careful preparation and personal sacrifice. Standing before God in the holiest place of all was a privilege that was to be taken with the utmost seriousness.

So it is with sex.

We are not to treat sex lightly and carelessly, as merely a

means to selfish gratification. It is not our "right" to have sex with whomever we want, whenever we want. Sex is not meant to be something we do on a casual whim. Rather, sex must be treated with as much reverence as the Jews treated the holiest place of the temple. When we express our love to someone physically, it is to be an act of the utmost intimacy, trust, vulnerability and selfless love.

Bottom line: if we want Great Sex, we must honor God's pattern by keeping sacred things sacred.

2. *A marriage covenant is God's chosen context for keeping sex sacred.* A marriage ceremony means far more than merely walking down the aisle, exchanging rings, and rattling off some formal-sounding words about our love and devotion toward another person. The Bible tells us, "Marriage is to be held in honor among all, and the marriage bed is to be undefiled, for fornicators and adulterers God will judge" (Heb. 13:4 NASB).

A marriage ceremony is a forging of one of the most sacred exchanges in all of Scripture—covenant. When you enter into a marriage covenant with your spouse, you are no longer your own; you are in holy covenant with your spouse, and your two lives have become one, forever. Sex is the outward expression of what takes place in a marriage covenant—it is an exchange of all that we have, all that we are, a complete surrendering of ourselves to another person. That is why we are to keep sex within the bounds of marriage—because it is meant to be a demonstration of holy covenant, not just a mere physical expression of affection and attraction.

This is God's perfect pattern.

We cannot experience an intimate relationship with God until a covenant has been made—an exchange of all that we are for all that He is. Only through covenant can we enter the holy of holies in our relationship with God.

The same is true for earthly romance. Only through covenant are we free to enter the "holy of holies" with another person and discover Great Sex as God intended it to be.

QUESTION: Is sex really better if you save it for marriage?

I was quite dubious when the guest speaker at my girls' Bible study tried to convince us that sex would be so much better if we waited until marriage. It didn't help that she was a serious, frumpy woman who seemed about as sexless as Blackstone's *Commentaries on the Law*. I had seen her, on occasion, with her husband, and their marriage didn't seem much different from the throngs of dour-faced couples who seemed to flock into church circles.

For all the hype and buildup about sex-God's-way being the most fulfilling, most of the Christians around me weren't very convincing. Other than my parents and a small handful of others, most Christian couples I observed as a young person didn't hold hands, kiss, smile at each other, speak sweetly to each other, or show any demonstration of a passionate love and fulfilling sex life. Hollywood, on the other hand, made casual, nonmarried sex look fun, romantic, exciting, and extremely satisfying. When it came down to the question of who was enjoying sex more, the evidence was strongly in favor of the just-do-it-right-now crowd.

It wasn't until my love story with Eric that I began to see things more clearly. In the Christian circles I grew up in, Purity had been completely misrepresented. Christian adults who seemed unhappy, or at least mediocre, in their own marriages were always trying to convince me that Purity was the prescription for fulfillment; yet I had grown up, along with most of my peers, secretly believing that Purity was a prescription for misery.

But then I encountered the *real* Mr. Purity—the strong, dignified, heroic being who exists not to rob us of fun and fulfillment, but to help us discover Great Sex in all its glory. Here is what Eric and I discovered with Mr. Purity as our guide: *Saving sex until marriage is not what makes it fulfilling—following God's perfect pattern for Great Sex is what makes it truly fulfilling.*

Modern Christian teaching on Purity often leads us to believe that sex will automatically be amazing, wonderful, and supremely satisfying if we save it until marriage. But there are plenty of married couples out there with miserable sex lives, despite the fact that they did not have sex before their wedding day. It's not the waiting itself that brings fulfillment and satisfaction to a couple's sex life; rather, it's following God's perfect, amazing pattern for Great Sex—honoring all four members of the League throughout our entire lives. Keeping sex within the confines of a marriage covenant is a very important part of God's pattern—but there's a lot more to His pattern than simply waiting for marriage.

At the core of Great Sex is a key principle—*selflessness.*

Sex in our modern culture, even among many Christians, has become the very opposite of a selfless, giving act. It has been turned into a selfish, flesh-gratifying "right" that we feel we deserve as soon as we say I do. But if we approach sex with a selfish attitude, we will never experience Great Sex as God intended it to be. Our sex lives will be no more fulfilling than those who gratify their desires before marriage. It's only when we selflessly lay down our lives for our spouse and allow sex to be an outflow of that sacrificial love that we truly experience the amazing satisfaction of physical intimacy in all its glory.

Saving sex until marriage should be something we do because we desire to honor our spouse and honor God's perfect pattern, not merely because we hope to get better sex in marriage. A marriage covenant means laying down our very lives for our spouse—declaring that all we have and all we are now belongs to him or her. And that is the attitude we must take into our marriage in order to experience Great Sex. We must orient our lives to seek our spouse's highest good—to consider our spouse first, above ourselves, with our time, resources, and actions. When sex stems from a selfless love, lifelong devotion, and holy covenant commitment, then and only then will we experience a version of sex that Hollywood can never touch. In God's perfect pattern, both spouses are free to fully give themselves to each other with abandon, because of the implicit love and trust that stems from their holy covenant relationship.

When a husband daily lays down his life for his wife, considers her needs above his own, and sacrifices his own agenda in order to be sensitive to her, he will truly become the man that she desires above any other. When a wife builds her existence around serving her husband, meeting his needs, and thinking of his good above her own, her man will respond with a radical adoration for her alone. That's what makes sex great. It's a pattern that begins long before the wedding day by taking Mr. Purity's hand, laying down our own selfish wants, and honoring God's context for sex. And if we continue in that pattern even after the vows are spoken, we'll be in for a passionate love story more perfect than anything this world could ever dream of.

(For more about developing selfless habits toward your spouse, we encourage you to read our book *The First 90 Days of Marriage*.[1])

QUESTION: What about second chances?

What if you have already taken sex out of God's context? Are you doomed to have a second-rate version of sex in marriage?

First, if you are asking that question, you are not alone. Too many of us have stumbled in this area and are left wondering if it is too late for us to encounter Great Sex through God's perfect pattern.

The answer to this question is a resounding, "No—it is not too late!" When we repent from our sin, God washes us clean, as white as snow. He does not punish us with a second-rate version of love and romance. Eric and I are living testimonies of the fact that we serve a God of new beginnings. Let your heart be encouraged by this excerpt from *When God Writes Your Love Story*:

The beauty of a God-written love story is not something reserved for the perfect and pious; it's for sinners like you and like me. That's what God's love is all about. We are so unworthy of His grace and forgiveness—and yet He offers it to us freely. If you have fallen in this area of your life and have asked yourself the question, 'Is it too late for me?' read

John 8:1–11 and take a close look at how Jesus responded to the woman caught in adultery. When we come to Him, bleeding and broken, filled with pain and regret, afraid to look into His eyes . . . He smiles tenderly. He lifts our chin with His nail-scarred hands. And He gently says, "I don't condemn you. Now go, and stop sinning."

When we come face to face with this perfect love, it takes our breath away. We deserve to die for what we have done. We should be stoned by an angry mob. But not only does Jesus save our life with His own blood, He washes us completely clean. When He looks at us, He doesn't see our failures and mistakes—He sees a new creation, a child of God.

He tells us to "go and sin no more." He is speaking of repentance. This is the act of humbling ourselves, confessing our sin, and determining in our heart to turn and walk away from our sin from this day forward. Repentance literally means turning from our sin and walking in the other direction. With His tender guiding hand in our lives, we can repent . . . and be made new. When we repent and accept His forgiveness, He can take the sin that our enemy meant to use to destroy us, and use it for His glory. He can take a shattered heart and life and script a beautiful tale of His perfect love.[2]

Be careful that you do not take this amazing gift of forgiveness lightly or use it as an excuse to live selfishly. Repentance is not merely confessing our sin, but *turning* from our sin. In other words, exchanging our old pattern of thinking for God's pattern, our old pattern of living for God's pattern. Offer Him your whole existence from this day forward, and you will be amazed at how faithful your God will be.

Many young people ask us how and when they should tell their future spouse about mistakes they have made in the past. There is no pat answer to this question. The most important thing is to be completely surrendered to God throughout the process and yielded to His Spirit. He will guide and direct if you allow Him to.

Eric and I sat down with each other about six months before we were engaged and confessed to each other the ways in which we had not honored each other in purity. I had expected it to be a traumatic conversation, but it was the opposite. As I looked into Eric's eyes, I saw complete forgiveness—the very love of Christ—looking back at me. God had enabled him to see me, not marred or tainted by my mistakes, but as a completely new creation in Christ, a radiant princess of purity. And as he confessed his own sins to me, I allowed the love of Christ to work through me and offer complete forgiveness. Never once have our past mistakes had any effect upon the purity and beauty of our love story. After that night of confession, we didn't even have the need to think about or speak about those things again. God gave us a fresh beginning. And we have never looked back.

That is the way it always is when Christ is at the center of a relationship. Instead of hurt, jealousy, and suspicion, there is full forgiveness and trust. And God takes what the enemy meant for evil in our lives and turns it into something that brings Him great glory and honor.

QUESTION: Is oral sex before marriage a sin in God's eyes?

Oral sex, in certain circles, has become known as *Christian sex*—seen by some as an expression of physical intimacy prior to marriage that is acceptable to God because it isn't the same as actually having sex.

Christians who engage in oral sex so they are still technical virgins on their wedding day are trying to have it both ways. They want to gratify their selfish, fleshly desires yet still reap all the benefits of God's pattern for Great Sex.

But it doesn't work that way. God's rewards don't come to those who are always looking for loopholes and asking, "How can I have my own way and stay on God's good side?" Rather, He honors those who are willing to lay down every selfish desire and seek His highest and best. He blesses those willing to live *without even a hint* of impurity in their lives.

It goes back to the ever-popular "How far is too far?" question. When we look for loopholes in God's pattern, we are not acting according to His nature. Rather than selflessly seeking to honor God and our future spouse by keeping sex as a sacred expression of the marriage covenant, we are asking how we can experience physical intimacy now and still reap the benefits of remaining pure until marriage.

Contrary to popular belief, having oral sex before marriage while abstaining from regular sex is not a sneaky way to have the best of both worlds; it's merely a sneaky way for Imposter Sex to gain greater control over your life.

To keep sex sacred, we must keep *all* expressions of sexual intimacy sacred. Sexual touch of any kind is an intimate knowing of another person—and such intimate acts, in God's pattern, are only meant as an outflow of a holy marriage covenant. When we read the Song of Solomon, we discover that it is not just the act of sex, *but all other forms of intimate touch and expression* that are reserved for the holy of holies alone. (Interesting side note: you will not find oral sex among the beautiful expressions of physical intimacy in God's perfect pattern, as outlined in the Song of Solomon. So if you are wondering whether oral sex even after marriage is appropriate, let that be your guide! We can never improve upon the way God designed a man and woman to express their love—our own methods will only warp and degrade it.)

When we choose the League as our companions, we choose a completely different pattern of living. Our lives exist to serve our King and to selflessly lay down our lives for our future spouse. No longer are we seeking to serve our own selfish wants or gratify the desires of our flesh. Eric and I chose not to even kiss until our wedding day. We wanted to go out of our way to keep every form of intimacy sacred. My dad had once told us, "Anything physically that you save for marriage will only be more beautiful and fulfilling as time goes on. Anything that you experience beforehand will eventually loose its luster." When we put this wisdom into practice, we found it to be true. Even to this very day, whenever we share a kiss it is just as beautiful, thrilling, and satisfying as it was on our wedding day.

Eric and I had grown up asking "How far is too far?" But we chose to start honoring God by asking a new question: "How far can I possibly go, Lord, to please and honor You in this area of my life?"

And as we made it our goal to live without even a hint of

impurity in our physical relationship, we discovered that God does indeed honor those who honor Him (1 Sam. 2:30). Because we saved everything in our physical relationship, it has only grown more and more amazing, fulfilling, and exciting with each year of our marriage. God's ways *are* perfect!

QUESTION: How does God feel about self-sex (masturbation)?

As we discussed earlier, Great Sex, in God's perfect design, stems from *selfless* devotion to another, not self-focused gratification of our own desires. The same principle applies here. Besides being an ugly, unpoetic word, masturbation is a self-focused attempt to gratify our own fleshly wants. At the very core of this act is selfishness, which goes against the nature of Christ and of God's perfect pattern for Great Sex.

In his first letter to the Corinthians, the apostle Paul writes, "What? know ye not that your body is the temple of the Holy Ghost which is in you, which ye have of God, and ye are not your own? For ye are bought with a price: therefore glorify God in your body, and in your spirit, which are God's" (1 Cor. 6:19–20).

When we surrender our life to Jesus Christ and claim Him as Lord, our body does not belong to us anymore. It is the domain of His Holy Spirit. And everything we do with our body is to bring honor to Him, *not* to gratify our own desires. We now serve Him, not ourselves. It is no longer our right to obey the voice of our flesh, acting for our own selfish pleasure. Rather, we are to be at His beck and call, continually asking the question, "How can I honor and please You, Lord, in every moment of every day?" Even in the smallest aspects of our lives, even in our most private moments, all is to be done for the glory of God, not the pleasure of our flesh. As Paul writes, "Whether therefore ye eat, or drink, or whatsoever ye do, do all to the glory of God" (1 Cor. 10:31).

We are asked to demonstrate God's glory (to honor and exalt Him) in *everything* we do—down to the smallest detail of our lives. Can you glorify God while masturbating? No! You are only glorifying and gratifying your own fleshly wants. Self-stimulation takes the beautiful gift of sexual pleasure and cheapens it into a shameful, secretive, animalistic impulse. It is devoid of the dignity, nobility, and divine romance that Sacred, Mr. Purity, and the rest of the League bring to Great Sex.

The Bible says, "For if ye live after the flesh, ye shall die: but if ye through the Spirit do mortify the deeds of the body, ye shall live" (Rom. 8:13). The "deeds of the body" means the selfish demands of our flesh for pleasure and gratification. Masturbation is a prime example of a selfish, fleshly demand of our body. God asks us to "mortify" those things, which literally means to "embalm" them, as in preparing a dead body for burial—in other words, put the deeds and desires of the flesh to death and make sure they *stay* dead.

In modern times, many of us have bought into the lie that frequent sexual release is a natural "need" of the body. We've come to believe that if we are not having sex, we at least have the right to gain release through self-stimulation. But God created only one context for sexual release—as an outflow of physical intimacy in a holy marriage covenant. Anything outside of that is unhealthy and unnatural. (Note to guys: unconscious nocturnal emissions that are not self-stimulated or associated with lustful thoughts are the one exception.)

Meet Mr. Smith

Yes, our sexual longings—the voice of our flesh—can be powerful and intense. But God's Spirit within us is far stronger. He will grant us the grace, the supernatural, enabling power, to honor Him with our body for as long as He has called us to a season of singleness.

The apostle Paul knew firsthand the struggles of singleness, but he also knew the importance of making sure his physical body didn't control his life. He told the Corinthians, "I discipline my body and bring it into subjection, lest, when I have preached to others, I myself should become disqualified" (1 Cor. 9:27).

Rather than allowing our physical bodies to rule us, God asks us to bring our bodies under subjection to His Spirit—we are not to be slaves to the wants of our bodies; we are to be slaves to His rulership over our lives. We are not to yield to the cries of our flesh, but to the call of our true Master, Jesus Christ. True, this is no easy task. But that is why we have the power of the God of the universe at our disposal!

QUESTION: Is lust really a big deal to God? Isn't it just a normal guy-thing?

God is clear about lust: "You have heard that it was said to those of old 'You shall not commit adultery.' But I say to you that whoever looks at a woman to lust for her has already committed adultery with her in his heart" (Matt. 27:28).

But in recent years, we have written off this command as unrealistic. *Christ didn't really mean that,* we say to ourselves. *I mean, He knows that we are only human. He understands that lust is just a weakness we will always deal with.*

Yet the truth is that Christ always means what He says. He desires us to be free from the tyranny of lust. He wants to train His men to view women through a completely different lens— to see them as valuable, priceless, princesses of purity. He wants to train guys to stand up and heroically protect purity, not to selfishly conquer it.

And what about girls? No longer is lust merely a guy problem. Too many young women have accepted lust into their lives as a normal part of sexuality. But the standard is no different for women—God requires absolutely purity of mind and heart. Not only that, but He expects us to protect the hearts and minds of guys by allowing Purity and Holiness to influence how we dress, speak, walk, flirt, and act. The Bible says that women are "to adorn themselves with proper clothing, modestly and discreetly" (1 Tim. 2:9 NASB).

Jesus Christ wants sparkling cleanliness in His children from the inside out. Not because He is a cruel, stern ruler attempting to make us miserable. Rather, because He is the very essence of love, and He desires for us to experience love as He created it to be—untainted by the destructive power of lust.

Lust and Purity have been arch rivals since sin came into the world. While Purity's role is to bring strength and nobility to a man's life, Lust's aim is to bring weakness and shame. Purity helps a man rise to the amazing heights of marvelous Manhood, while Lust keeps a man trapped and enslaved to mediocrity and selfishness.

Modern culture is a huge support to Lust's agenda. Boys from the time they are in elementary school are taught that in order to be a "normal" guy they have to be obsessed with sex. Guys today usually grow up believing that Lust is just a part of the male chemistry. But Lust is not a normal guy trait. God intends a man to be victoriously, triumphantly free from the power of Lust—to view women with complete dignity and respect in every situation. To keep his mind, heart, and body set-apart for one woman alone—his wife.

The same is true for women. Girls are taught by the culture that unless guys are lusting after them, they are not truly beautiful. So instead of protecting and guarding the purity of a man's mind, they attempt to conquer it with seduction, immodesty, and flirting. But God does not want women to accept the "guys will be guys" attitude. He wants women to challenge men to His standard and to do everything they can to help men be transformed into princes of purity.

And it is important to note that men are not the only ones who struggle with their thought lives. Sexual fantasies, impure thoughts, and even looking at pornography is a vice for all too many young women today. This should never be shrugged off as if they are merely exploring their "normal" sexual desires. God has so much more for His daughters than a mind given over to the warped imaginations of Lust.

We must not accept Lust as a casual part of our lives. Rather, through the enabling power of God, we are to wipe out any trace of it. Let us no longer listen to the voices of modern culture, telling us that lust is normal. Rather, let us heed the very standard of Almighty God.

Job said, "I made a covenant with my eyes not to look with lust upon a young woman. . . . For lust is a shameful sin, a crime that should be punished. It is a devastating fire that destroys to hell. It would wipe out everything I own" (Job 31:1, 11–12). When we allow Lust into our lives, we are playing with a destructive fire that threatens both our spiritual and physical lives. When we adopt God's attitude toward Lust, we are on our way to becoming the heroic men and women He created us to be, not enslaved to the ways of this world, but servants of a higher kingdom.

QUESTION: Should men be the initiators in a relationship?

I have yet to meet a woman who is longing for a weak, wimpy, insecure man who never takes the lead or makes decisions. One of the biggest cries of young unmarried women today is, "Where are all the men?" Instead of strong, confident leaders who reflect the manhood of Mr. Marvelous, they see insecure followers—guys who don't seem to have a backbone and don't seem to even know how to pursue a woman's heart. Unfortunately, women aren't helping the problem.

When a woman tries to take a man's role in a relationship, she robs him of his masculine strength. Sure, he may at first appear to like it when a woman pursues him. After all, it saves him the insecurity of sticking his neck out or having to go to all the effort of carefully winning her heart. He may be temporarily flattered by her aggression toward him, but in the end, he will lose respect for both her and his own masculinity. Instead of becoming her protector and leader, he will become lazy and lackluster, expecting her to do all the work in the relationship.

On the flip side, if a woman allows a man to rise to the challenge of pursuing her, wooing her, and winning her heart over time, instead of thrusting it upon him too readily—his masculine strength will be tested and strengthened. Once he has pursued and won his prize according to God's perfect pattern, he is far less likely to take her for granted. Rather, he will become the heroic protector he was created to be—laying down his life to preserve and nurture the heart of the princess that he worked so hard to win.

A strong, confident, heroic man who rises to the challenge of winning a woman's heart and then carefully protects and preserves his hard-won prize . . . this is the ultimate romantic desire of nearly every woman I have ever talked to. Yet, ironically, many women are actually robbing men of these qualities simply by their own impatience. They are in such a hurry to snag a man that they don't wait for him to initiate. They take the lead, become the pursuer instead of the pursued, and in so doing they strip their man of all the strong masculine qualities they so desire him to have.

I struggled with this problem greatly during my single years. Growing up, my parents exhorted me over and over again that men were more attracted to women who allowed the guy to take the lead—but to me it seemed that the aggressive girls were the ones to get all the male attention. I wondered, *If I wait for a guy to pursue me, how can I be sure that anyone ever will? Isn't this idea of men needing to be the initiator an outdated concept anyway?*

Even in my blossoming friendship with Eric, this question plagued me. As our friendship progressed, it seemed obvious that something more was developing between us—and yet he did not initiate a conversation about it. So I waited. I prayed. I came close so many times to initiating a conversation about where the friendship was going. But God's Spirit continued to hold me back.

Finally, when the time was right, Eric took the lead. And one of the first things he said to me was how much it meant to him that I had allowed him to be the one to initiate a conversation about our relationship. "You respected my position as a man," he told me, "and not many girls today would do that."

Even when Eric expressed feelings for me that went beyond friendship, I felt God caution me not to offer my heart to him too readily or quickly. With God's gentle and faithful direction, I opened my heart to Eric slowly, gradually, as he proved by his honor, respect, and integrity that he was worthy of such a gift. He did not respond to my hesitation with impatience or disgust. Rather, he rose to the challenge and seemed to respect me all the more as I protected and guarded my feminine mystique. And as a result, I felt like a princess being pursued by a gallant prince.

We can only experience the absolute beauty, sacredness, and perfection of God's perfect pattern for romance when we fulfill the masculine and feminine roles He created for us.

One of the biggest complaints I hear from married women is that the husband doesn't take a leadership position in the marriage—which often leads to a lot of fruitless nagging and criticizing on the wife's part. Quite often, the problem in these marriages emerged long before the wedding day, at the very beginning of the relationship. The woman took the lead, became the initiator, and stepped into the role that God designed the man to be in. Then the unhealthy pattern was carried into the marriage relationship, setting the stage for ustration and disillusionment.

'irls, if you desire your future husband to be a strong, confident leader in your marriage, then let the relationship begin according to God's pattern. Allow the man to be the initiator, the leader, and the pursuer. And guys, it may be more work for you to step into the role that God designed you for, but if you are willing to rise to the challenge, you will be amazed at how your masculine strength will soar. Don't just settle for an easy girl who throws her heart at you without a fight. Set your sights on the girl who is guarding and protecting her feminine mystique. Yes, it will be more effort to win her heart—but a hard-won prize is infinitely more valuable than something casually offered and easily gained.

One of my good friends, Natalie, had a close guy friend, Jason, whom she respected and admired very much. They seemed to share a connection that went beyond mere friendship, and Natalie was unable to shake the strong feeling that this man could be God's intended future husband for her. But years went by, and still Jason did not initiate anything more than friendship. At times he seemed interested in something more, but he never made any move in that direction.

"Why shouldn't I just initiate a conversation with him about how I feel?" she wondered many times. "What's so wrong with just being open and honest about what I think God might be doing between us?" But after much prayer, she decided that she would leave it in God's hands. "If God wants us to be together, He is perfectly capable of prompting Jason to take the lead."

Finally, after Natalie had all but given up on the hope of a relationship ever happening, Jason approached her. He told her that he felt God leading him to pursue a romantic relationship with her, and he expressed his gratitude that she had waited patiently for him to take the lead. He began to pursue her heart, and when he had fully won it, he cherished it with everything in him. It became a beautiful, sacred, God-glorifying relationship. And it started with True Femininity allowing True Masculinity to shine.

"If I had rushed ahead with my own agenda," she told me later, "I would have missed out on the greatest gift that God had for me. I allowed Jason to be the man in our relationship. And now, he treats me like a princess—he stands up for me, protects me, and honors me in every way. I am so glad I followed God's pattern!"

God's ways can often seem old-fashioned in our modern mode of thinking. But His pattern never becomes outdated and His ways never go out of style. God's pattern restores the long-lost art of masculine nobility and feminine dignity—returning us to the days of gallant lords and fair maidens. Every guy wants to be a heroic prince; every girl wants to be a beautiful princess. Following God's design for True Manhood and True Femininity is what sets the stage for those seemingly impossible dreams to actually come true. If finding our deepest romantic longings fulfilled is what comes of following God's design—then I think we need more of His amazing *old fashioned* ways!

QUESTION: What does God think about flirting?

In modern relationships, flirting seems about as innocent and harmless as window-shopping at the mall. "What's the harm of browsing, as long as you don't actually buy anything?" a young man once asked us during a discussion on the topic.

Even young people who have chosen God's pattern for relationships and are seeking to live a set-apart life for their future spouse often shrug off flirting as a natural part of any male-female interaction. But take a closer look at what flirting really is, and it becomes clear that some important principles in God's pattern are violated by doing it.

Flirting is, in essence, drawing another person's attention toward *you*. It is using your masculine or feminine power to entice another person to notice, admire, and be attracted to you. It is putting your personality, body, humor, and wit on display—playing a game in which you score more points the more positive attention you receive from the other person.

Flirting, at its core, is based on selfishness.

If Eric flirted with other women, I would be hurt, jealous, and angry. If I flirted with other men, he would feel outraged and betrayed. We are in a covenant marriage relationship, and we have pledged to have eyes only for each other. I belong to Eric—mind, body, and heart. And he belongs to me. We honor each other by keeping our attentions sacred—reserved for our spouse alone. Most would agree that this is the way it should be.

If then, as a married person you would not dishonor or hurt your spouse by flirting with anyone else—why would you hurt your future spouse now by flirting with others *before* marriage? If you have chosen to set your life aside for the person you will one day marry, then the "two-eyeball" principle must be applied when it comes to flirting. If your future spouse were standing beside you, seeing you interact with the opposite sex, how would he or she feel? Once you ask that question and answer honestly, flirting no longer becomes a harmless, innocent activity.

There is another aspect of flirting that violates God's perfect pattern. When two people are in a relationship with God at the center, they always seek to draw the other person closer to Him, not to each other. Whether before or after marriage, a God-scripted love story is one in which each person is seeking to point the other toward Christ, not merely toward themselves.

My own relationship past was checkered with plenty of shallow, selfish, temporary relationships based around trying to impress another person. But my relationship with Eric was completely different. Even from the time we were new friends, it was Eric's goal to point me toward Jesus Christ and not draw me to himself. As a result, after spending time with him, my thoughts were on Christ, and my desire was to know Jesus more.

As our relationship progressed, this pattern only continued. Instead of playing with my emotions and drawing my affections toward himself, Eric constantly spoke of Christ, exhorted me toward Christ, and displayed the unselfish nature of Christ. And when Eric eventually sat down with my dad to talk about the relationship, my dad told him, "The reason I know that your friendship with my daughter is from God is because ever since you have been in her life, she has drawn closer to Jesus Christ." It became the foundation for our entire love story and marriage relationship—instead of drawing Eric to myself, my goal is to draw him more to Christ—and vice versa. And ironically, as we point each other closer to Christ, we naturally draw closer to each other.

Eric expounded upon this principle in our book, *A Perfect Wedding*:

When John the Baptist said the words, "He (Jesus) must increase, but I must decrease," (John 3:30) he was using terminology that a Jew would understand in the context of a wedding covenant.

Most of us read about John the Baptist in the Bible, find his story interesting, but then move on through the text, never realizing the amazing applicability of his example to our marriages. John the Baptist is one of the most profound pictures of what God designed marriage to be. God asks each of us, as a spouse, to be a "Friend of the Bridegroom"— to be a "forerunner" in our spouse's life to prepare the way for them to understand and apprehend Christ in all His fullness and glory.

Contrary to our typical way of thinking, marriage isn't about two people in love vowing to live in faithfulness 'til death parts them. Marriage is about two people serving each other, preparing each other for a Heavenly spouse, the ultimate Bridegroom, Jesus Christ.

Marriage is a constant choice to decrease so that Christ may increase in your spouse's life. Long and short, marriage is about Christ, more and more and more of Christ every day for an entire life long. When both spouses choose to befriend the Heavenly Bridegroom, the natural result is a romantic and poetic love for all time.[3]

When it comes to interaction with the opposite sex, our goal should be to put God's perfect pattern in place, to lay the foundation *even now* for a truly Christ-centered love story. In every friendship or relationship, if we constantly say, "I must decrease, so that Christ would increase," not only will we protect the sacredness of our love story, we will become shining examples of Christ's kingdom to this world around us. The Christian life is not all about us—it is all about *Him*!

If you aren't exactly sure where the line is between flirting and friendliness, ask God's Spirit to guide and direct you as you interact with the opposite sex. Allow Him to search your heart and motives, and reveal any selfish behavior pattern—no matter how small—that you have allowed to creep into your life. When in doubt, err on the side of caution. Remember, it's not about asking, "Where is the line?" but "How far can I possibly go to honor God and my future spouse in this area of my life?"

Giving up flirting can cause feelings of doubt and insecurity—as if the opposite sex won't ever notice you unless you are out there "playing the game." Allow God to prove Himself faithful. He is perfectly capable of bringing a love story into your life in His own time and way—without selfish manipulation on your part. And a love story initiated and developed by the Author of romance is far more fulfilling than one you manipulate on your own.

QUESTION: What if my parents don't approve of the relationship I am in?

Whether we like it or not, God placed parents in a very important role of authority over our lives. They are anointed by heaven to protect, provide for, and nurture us physically, emotionally, and physically. Even when we become independent and grown up, our parents still have a spiritual "sixth sense" for our lives; often seeing things that we ourselves cannot see. If your parents are not supportive of a decision in your life, you would be wise to take their concern seriously. Parents (and others who are in spiritual authority over our lives) can serve as rearview and sideview mirrors for us. They can see the dangers that we, in the driver's seat, might miss without their input.

When parents seem to be unreasonable and overprotective, our first instinct is to pull away and make our own decisions, keeping them at arm's length from the important areas of our lives. But often their seemingly unreasonable statements and overprotective attitudes simply stem from the fact that they feel left out—they are merely grasping for the position that God meant them to have; as wise counselors and teammates in the life of their children. If you will invite them to participate as teammates in your life—especially in the area of relationships—you will likely find that they will become far less "concerned" and far more supportive, simply because their position in your life has been honored and respected. I found this to be true in my own love story with Eric.

Though I never would have been excited about the idea of having my parents involved in my love story—it turned out to be one of the most beautiful aspects of my relationship with Eric. As I invited my parents to pray for me and share their wisdom with me, they truly became teammates—not just figures of authority. They deeply desired the best for this area of my life, and I found that they were not overbearing or overprotective—they simply offered wise counsel and advice, and served as a wonderful sounding board whenever I needed to process things that were happening.

Eric honored my dad's position by receiving his blessing before the relationship even began. And every few weeks he and my dad would meet together to talk about the relationship and discuss ways Eric could be more sensitive toward me. What woman wouldn't feel like a princess with the two most important men in her life getting together on a regular basis to talk about how they can be sensitive to her?

Honoring my parents in our relationship brought security, stability, and even romance—and to this day our parents are among our best friends.

Of course, not all parents can serve this role. Those who are not walking with God may be incapable of becoming wise spiritual counselors and prayer partners. But even then, as much as you can honor and respect their position in your life—you should do so. As we honor our parents, God honors us. If your parents are not walking with God and you feel that you need stronger spiritual teammates, pray that He would bring other people into your life who can fill that position—whether it be a pastor, biblical counselor, or respected Christian friend. It's a prayer that He loves to answer. Navigating your way through the confusing waters of relationship building is far smoother with teammates to help guide you.

If you find that, even after inviting your parents to be on your team, they are still not on board about a relationship that you are in, or one you are thinking about pursuing, here is what Eric and I suggest:

1. *Talk It Out.* Sit down with your parents for a long period of time, when you won't be interrupted, and really listen to their concerns. Don't use this time for explaining your point of view

or becoming defensive; simply seek to understand the reasons behind their hesitation. Listen to their words with an open heart and mind, allowing God to show you anything that He might want to speak to you through what they have to say.

2. *Take It to God.* Take some time away from the relationship and pray for God's perspective and wisdom. (If you feel that the relationship is one that you cannot step away from, even for a season, then that's probably a sign that it has an unhealthy position in your life anyway. God is perfectly capable of holding a relationship together during a time of separation, if that is His desire for your life.) God is a rewarder of those who diligently seek Him (Heb. 11:6). Pray that if this relationship is His will for your life, He would change your parents' hearts. Pray that if He does not desire the relationship, He will give you complete peace about walking away. Allow God to speak, rather than simply rushing ahead with your own agenda and desires.

God is a big God. Trust Him to work supernaturally through the teammates He has placed in your life to guide and direct your path.

Of course, sometimes parents can take the pen out of God's hands and try to manipulate their child's life out of their own selfishness, pride, or fear. If you sense that happening in your situation, give God a chance to change their hearts. And if He does not, then simply make the best decision you know how to make before God. If you truly desire His guidance and direction, He will not allow you to miss it. But be sure that the motive of your heart is to glorify and honor Him, even above your own desires.

QUESTION: What if I'm in a relationship with a girl who doesn't want to kiss until the wedding?

Guys, if you are blessed enough to find a young woman who deeply values sacred things, you should fall upon your knees and thank God. You have been given a rare and priceless gift that few men in today's world ever find. Now is your opportunity to place your own selfish desires aside and heroically stand up as a protector of your woman's purity. If you will preserve and honor her desires, rather than evaluating them based on your own wants, you will be on your way to becoming an incredible husband—a demonstration of Jesus Christ, who laid down His very life for His Bride. And your girl will glow with respect and admiration for you, her heroic protector.

Once a woman makes it clear to a man what her physical and emotional boundaries are, it is his sacred duty to protect those boundaries at all costs. In the heat of emotion she might change her mind, but the true test of his manhood will come when he protects them anyway—at the expense of his own desires. If a man allows a woman to violate her boundaries prior to marriage, no matter how harmless it may seem at the time, the woman will carry resentment and disrespect toward him into their marriage.

A woman is longing for a man who will rise up and heroically protect her purity, rather than selfishly entice her to lower her standards. As Eric says in his book *God's Gift to Women*:

A woman doesn't just want her man to *understand* her sacred boundary line—she wants him to *heroically pro-*

tect it. A woman desires her man to protect what is sacred within her—her physical and emotional purity. She doesn't just want him to gruntingly agree not to violate her boundary line. She wants him to eagerly protect the purity of their physical and emotional relationship together.

As guys we haven't been trained to protect femininity, we've been trained only to conquer it. But the essence of a Christ-built warrior isn't just overcoming difficult obstacles (i.e. women with morals) but rather to *become* a difficult obstacle, standing in the way of all forms of impurity and injustice. A warrior doesn't complain about sacred boundary lines—*he gives his life to protect them.*[4]

So once again, guys, if you are blessed enough to have a girl who values purity and feminine mystique, stop complaining! Now is your chance to become the kind of Christ-like, heroic warrior of her dreams who proves himself truly worthy of her heart.

And don't worry—just because your fiancé doesn't want to kiss until your wedding does *not* mean she'll be "sexually frigid" after the wedding day. When two people follow God's perfect pattern for Great Sex—including absolute purity before the wedding day—they discover physical intimacy in all its glory. Honor and respect your girl's desires for purity, love her with an unselfish and Christlike love, and she will offer her entire self to you without reserve when the moment comes.

Bonus Questions

Unfortunately, there are a few doozy questions I wasn't able to fit in this book, but I have made the answers available online. Go to www.meetmistersmith.com and look under the section entitled *bonus questions* if you are interested in our answers to the following questions:

- What kind of physical touch is appropriate in a premarriage relationship?
- What are healthy physical and emotional boundaries for guy–girl friendships?
- What should I do about my sexual addictions?
- How does God feel about homosexuality? Aren't some people born that way?

If after reading the questions in this book and those available online, you still have additional questions, feel free to submit additional questions for Eric and me to answer at www.setapartlife.com/mistersmith.

CHAPTER 20

Doing It the
Old-Fashioned Way

Have you ever wished to live in sixteenth-century England? Honor, nobility, chivalry—they were all there. People seemed to think loftier thoughts back then with a more majestic language at their disposal. Sure, they had dysentery and drafty living rooms and no refrigeration, but let's not focus on that part. There was a sense of decorum, a sense of honor, a sense of mystique.

The words *my lady* were spoken by gentlemen who laid their coats over mud puddles, instead of the words *hey babe*, spoken by gutless, sex-twisted men interested in only one thing. It almost makes you want to exchange your central heating and microwaves for a little more dignity.

Eric and I take this stuff seriously. You see, we believe that honor, nobility, chivalry, decorum, and mystique are attributes of purity and holiness. They are behaviors from a more regal realm, a nobler land.

People today seem to think that the more disgusting we are,

the more socially acceptable we become. We cheat, lie, and mishandle sacred things as if we were pigs seeing pearls as of no greater value than pebbles in the mud. We sit in front of televisions day and night, scream like banshees when footballs fly between two uprights, and with fingers covered in orange Cheetos dust, we shake hands with guests arriving for the party.

What's happened to us? Why do we excuse this animal behavior as if it were normal? Do we not represent the King of the universe?

It's bad enough that young men in our culture see these animalistic behaviors as manly, but it is even more shocking to see young girls being trained to burp, scratch, and emit foul odors as if this were the new version of hip femininity.

Eric and I believe that God's rendition of life is 180 degrees in the opposite direction—it's tasteful and dignified, stately and grand. We believe God's design speaks with a more majestic tone and that it walks with a regal gait. It is not pompous, but rather humbly chivalrous and lovingly elegant.

When Eric writes me love notes, he adds in a few *thous* and *thees*—and you know what? I like it. It makes me feel like a lady when he says to me, "Thou art my dearest Leslie!" Now, for clarification, Eric doesn't speak in thous and thees to the exclusion of making any sense; rather, he provides the perfect blend of sense and sensibility. He takes a higher language and a nobler manner and blends it into our modern world. And that is what I think is necessary today.

We all need to add more nobility to our behavior, more majesty to our language, more elegance to our presentation, and more sacred decorum to our bearing. I realize that we don't live in sixteenth-century England and that adding too much sentiment might make us appear as if we are kooks attempting to live in a bygone era. But I say it is high time that we do something about the burping, scratching mannerisms of our modern times.

Mr. Purity, Sacred, Mr. Marvelous, and Feminine Grace are all of a more refined nature. They are noble, chivalrous, decorous, mysterious, and supremely dignified. And so is the version of sex that they cook up. Great Sex is not the act of animals but the physically lived out love poetry of a prince and a princess.

I realize that our views on sexuality might sound a bit old fashioned for your tastes. Maybe you prefer the loose sexuality of our time, the lack of commitment, the loss of gender definitions, and the absence of dignity and decorum, but I would challenge you to make sure you don't call "old-fashioned" what God merely calls correct. God is not an "old-fashioned" God; He is the same yesterday, today, and forever. He invented Great Sex, and He is the only one who can actually help us find it.

If you are looking for quick thrills, popularity, and worldly applause, I'm afraid we can't provide you a lot of help. But if you are interested in a life of supreme satisfaction and unequalled liberty and happiness, then this book has everything you need to get started.

I'm a girly girl, and growing up I always wished to play a part in a romantic Jane Austen novel. But I am blissfully happy living in this modern world with my Prince Beefy. I wouldn't even consider trading the beauty and romance of my current reality with Eric for a free ticket to be transported, in actuality, into that Jane Austen dreamland. I have found all the charm and enchantment of that "happily ever after" world right here and right now.

In fact, I will finish with these ten words:

Next to my husband, Mr. Darcy looks like a putz.

Taking the Purity Test

Most of us who have grown up in the Christian church can relate to Deuce's view of Purity. It's easy to see Purity as a wimpy, dirty, unpopular, annoying guy to be avoided at all costs. The problem is, as Christians, we can't completely avoid Purity. Unlike Deuce, who kept a healthy distance, we have to put up with Purity, at least to some extent, if we want to live an upright Christian life. For the typical Christian young person, Purity is a lot like that irritating, snot-nosed cousin your parents forced you to play with at family reunions. You couldn't stand him, but you had to grit your teeth and put up with him a few times a year because of your family.

That's how most Christians see Purity—as an annoying obligation. We can't understand why a loving God would subject His children to the inconveniences Purity brings. Because of Purity, we can't experience the thrill of sex before marriage without a guilty conscience, like everyone else seems to. Our popularity and worldly appeal becomes shaky and unstable—all because of that irritating little cousin called Purity who follows us around everywhere trying to embarrass us.

Take a moment to think about your view of Purity. Do you see him as God does? Do you marvel at his majesty, dignity, and strength? Are you eager for him to train and equip you to discover Great Sex? Or do you see him as an annoying obligation—someone to put up with in private, but not to be caught dead with in public?

The way you answer that question will define your ability to discover Great Sex.

Mr. Purity wants to test and prove you in the deepest part of your soul. He wants to train you to become a man or woman truly worthy of God's greatest treasures. Even if you have scorned Purity, mocked him, avoided him, or completely disregarded him, he is willing to come back into your life and remake you. All it takes is offering yourself fully and completely to Jesus Christ, asking Him to forgive and cleanse you from your sin, and by His grace, turning and walking a new way. Purity is one of the greatest gifts God ever bestowed upon His children.

If you are ready to encounter Purity the way God intended, here are some practical ways to begin.

1. *Pledge Allegiance to a New Master.* One of the reasons we often see Purity through a tainted lens is that Selfishness (Jimmy the Shrimp; the Flesh) is still ruling our existence. The Shrimp will do everything in his power to warp our view of God and make us afraid of turning over our existence to the King of all kings.

Jimmy the Shrimp is a liar. "You can't trust that old crusty tyrant!" the Shrimp howls in our ear. "All He wants to do is destroy your happiness and make you miserable!"

Even after we accept Christ as our Savior, the Shrimp is hard at work, attempting to keep us looking out for number one. "Sure, you have Christ now," he croons. "That's good fire insurance. Believing in Jesus will keep you out of hell. But don't take this Christianity thing too seriously. You can live for yourself, have fun, and enjoy life like everyone else does, and still go to heaven in the end! You can have it all!"

The moment we listen to the Shrimp's lies and start trying to "have it all"—to live for our own selfish pleasure and keep Christ merely as fire insurance—is the moment that we become blind to God's amazing kingdom pattern. Instead of seeing Purity as the glorious gift that he is, we think of him as an annoying obligation to put up with. When we distance ourselves from Purity, we distance ourselves from God and miss out on the incredible life He designed for us to live.

The only way to silence the Shrimp is to pledge allegiance to a new master. Instead of being ruled by our selfish desires, we must allow the Spirit of God to take the rulership position over our lives.

In February 1990, I knelt beside my bed and prayed, "Lord, take all of me. Have Your way. I lay everything at Your feet— my hopes, dreams, plans, desires, expectations, and longings. No longer do I live for myself; I live for You alone." Though I had technically been a Christian for many years, it was when I allowed God's Spirit to rule my existence that Purity was ushered into my life for the very first time.

It is when we possess a fully surrendered heart that Mr. Purity can become all God intended him to be in our lives. In our own strength, we cannot invite Purity to guide our existence. We can grit our teeth and squint our eyes, but without God's enabling power we will only see Purity as that annoying cousin and nothing more. Only when the Spirit of God rules our existence can Purity be ushered into our lives in all his muscular glory.

If you desire to be trained by the real Mr. Purity, there is a price to pay. It will cost your entire life—giving up control to a new Master. But, like I said in chapter 2, you aren't really the one in control of your life, anyway—Selfishness is. And wouldn't you rather be ruled by the King of the universe than a conniving weasel like Jimmy the Shrimp?

2. *Let Purity Test You.* Just as he did with me, Purity wants to make a "deal" with you. Only when you lay your soul bare before God and allow Purity to test you at the deepest level will you be ready for the journey toward Great Sex.

Lay your life before God and say, along with David the Psalmist, "Search me, O God, and know my heart: try me, and know my thoughts: And see if there be any wicked way in me, and lead me in the way everlasting" (Ps. 139:23–24). Allow Him to expose any patterns in your life that are selfish rather than Christ honoring, and then give you the grace to turn and walk a different way. Do not compare your existence to other Christians in your life. Our standard is the righteousness of Christ alone. Yes, to live a life of real purity is impossible, by human means. But that is why God desires to give us the very power of Christ working within us—to accomplish in and through our lives what we could never do on our own.

When it comes to romance and relationships, it is all too

easy to be self-serving and allow the Shrimp to worm his way back into a control position. Let God reveal any self-serving patterns in this area of your life, as you evaluate the following questions before Him:

- Do you chase after temporary relationships and sensual pleasure?
- Do you draw the attention of the opposite sex to yourself instead of to Christ?
- Do you surround yourself with the pleasures of the world, and secretly resent your commitment to Purity?
- Do you fill your mind with movies, music, and images that promote the twisted agenda of Imposter Sex?
- Do you see Imposter Sex the way God does—as a slimy wannabe—or are you allowing the culture to fool you into seeing him as desirable?
- Are you taking the "pen" of your life into your own hands and attempting to script your own love story, or are you fully allowing the Author of romance to do His amazing work?

And don't stop at relationship issues. As I said earlier, I thought I knew the full extent of Purity in my life. After all, Leslie and I had already allowed him to be a key player in the formation of our love story. But as I allowed Purity to test me through the course of writing this book, he exposed selfish blind spots—remnants of the Shrimp's control—that I didn't even know were there.

Take some time to prayerfully consider the following questions:

Meet Mr. Smith

- What position does prayer have in your life?
- Are you expecting God to do amazing things in your life without spending time in His presence?
- Are you disappointed that God doesn't seem to be coming through for you, yet you never give Him a chance to prove His faithfulness?
- Are you overlooking those who are weaker than you?
- Does your heart weep for the things God weeps for?
- Does your heart delight in the things God delights in?

Allow God's searchlight to probe deeply. Purity cannot be allowed to do his refining work in us until we first admit that we are not where we should be. The testing may be painful, but as you allow God to gently expose and straighten the crooked patterns in your life, He will make you truly worthy of the companionship of one so noble and grand as Mr. Purity.

3. *Start Asking a New Question.* If you were part of a church youth group, you probably remember the question posed in almost every discussion on sex: "How far is too far?" Most youth pastors answer that question by attempting to offer helpful guidelines about physical touch in guy-girl relationships. But the truth is "How far is too far?" is not a Christian question at all; it's a Jimmy the Shrimp question, based on selfishness.

If we want to lay the foundation for Great Sex, we can't approach Purity looking for loopholes. We will never reap the full blessings of God when we are wondering how *little* of Purity's training we can get by with. The only way to welcome the real Mr. Purity into our lives is to start asking a new question: "Lord Jesus, *how far can I possibly go* to please and honor You in this area of my life?"

In her book *God's Missionary*, Amy Carmichael stresses the importance of asking the right question.

> Ours must not be the love that asks "how little?" but "how much?" We must look upon the world, with all its delights and all its attractions, with suspicion and reserve. We are called to a higher Kingdom, we are touched with a diviner Spirit. It is not that He forbids us this or that comfort or indulgence; it is not that He is stern, demanding us to follow a narrow path. But we who love our Lord and whose affections are set on Heavenly things voluntarily and gladly lay aside the things that charm and ravish the world, that, for our part, our hearts may be ravished with the things of Heaven that our whole being may be poured forth in constant and unreserved devotion in the service of the Lord who died to save us.[1]

That's Purity in a nutshell. Purity's work causes us to approach every decision, every choice with a new question burning in our hearts. Instead of, "What is best for me?" we ask, "What is best for the fame and renown of God?" Once you start asking that question, your life will never be the same again. In fact, many of the seemingly confusing relationship questions that plague our generation can be answered by asking that one simple question.

If you live for the fame and renown of God and not the service of your selfish desires, then you will become one of Purity's most celebrated protégés.

Taking the Sacred Test

Allow God to show you the Sacred waiting opportunities He has placed in *your* life. All of those challenges you complain and gripe about could very well be strategic gifts for you to experience Sacred at her best. For instance, waiting for God to script your love story should never be a miserable, impatient, frustrating endeavor. If you allow Sacred to do her work, waiting for your spouse becomes a beautiful, exciting, set-apart season in which you become equipped and prepared for lifelong love.

If you desire to cultivate the lost art of Sacredness into your future love story, here are some practical ways to make it happen:

1. *Write Sacred Love Letters.* In our book *When God Writes Your Love Story*, Leslie and I wrote about our seasons of singleness, trusting God to bring our spouse into our life in His own perfect time and way.[1] A season of trust and waiting is not without cost.

While my friends were out with their significant others on the weekends, I often found myself alone with God—wondering how I would ever get married if I wasn't aggressively pursuing the opposite sex. Valentine's Day, New Year's Eve, and myriad other romantic opportunities came and went, and I found myself battling loneliness and an intense desire to have someone to hold in my arms.

That's when Sacred began to instruct me in the art of channeling all my romantic dreams and desires into expressions of love for my future spouse. I began to write her love letters. But not just a few hastily scribbled notes on torn pieces of notebook paper. *Real* love letters. You know, the old-fashioned kind—the kind where each word is specially chosen and every line dances across the page like happy poetry. The kind of letters that expressed my absolute devotion to protect the sacredness of a God-written love story. Whenever I began to feel lonely, impatient, and sorely tempted to run out and strike up a quick-fix relationship with the first girl I met, I would instead pour those desires into love for my future wife by penning these sacred love letters to her.

The more thought, time, energy, and effort I put into the letters, the more sacred my relationship with my future wife became. No longer did this woman merely exist in theory. Through my expressions of love to her, she became real to me. I pictured her reading these letters one day, her eyes lighting up with delight as she noticed every careful detail I had poured into each line, a smile creasing her face as she appreciated my amateur attempts at fine poetry. And I began to love her, even before meeting her. I began to have the strength to wait for something beautiful, something infinitely better than the haphazard, casual version of romance that most of my friends had settled for. And guess what? It was more than worth the wait.

On our honeymoon, I gave Leslie a notebook full of all the love letters I had written to her over the years—the expressions of romance I had crafted for her long before I even knew her name. As I watched her cherish every word and her eyes light up with delight over my love, devotion, and affection for her, I knew that Sacred had done her job well. Penning beautiful love letters to each other is a sacred part of our romance even now, after twelve years of marriage. What started as a simple seed of love for someone I'd never met has grown into a garden of romantic delight for someone I now share life with every day. One thing is certain about Sacred. Just like my lovely wife, when she is appreciated and nurtured, she becomes more beautiful with every passing year.

2. *Adopt a Sacred Code of Honor.* Inviting Sacred to shape our dealings with the opposite sex can either be something we grit our teeth and endure, or something that is noble, exciting, and beautiful. It all depends on whether she is honored in the process. The secret ingredient that makes the romance of the fairy tales so magical and the nobility of knights and fair maidens so desirable is something I call the lost art of *sacred honor.* Sacred honor means precisely what it sounds like it should mean—honoring the things that God designed to be sacred.

We live in a world that celebrates all things casual—casual sex, casual friendships, casual relationships, causal flirting, and even casual worship of God. Sacred things are no longer treated with reverence and respect; they are treated with haphazard carelessness. To bring back the beauty of romance, we must bring back the lost art of sacred honor.

Think about your future spouse. She will one day give you the gift of her heart—her trust, her respect, and her vulnerability. He will one day entrust his mind and body to you alone. Will you prove worthy of such a sacred treasure? Will you treat this holy gift, even now, with the delicacy and care it deserves?

No one around you may understand your sacred code of honor; the code that holds you back from flirting with the opposite sex, that keeps you from toying with their emotions, that causes you to wait for God's perfect timing instead of rushing ahead to fulfill your own impatient desires. To others, your code may seem unnecessary and extreme. But if you live by this code, you will usher the most glorious nobility, dignity, and strength into your love story; something that others only dream about but never experience in real life. You will become a gallant knight or heroic princess, defying everything in this unromantic, undignified world that declares fairy tales to be extinct.

I sometimes picture an inspiring movie score playing behind me as I go about my day. I realize that may seem a bit sappy to some, but I don't care. My imaginary movie score reminds me of the grand adventure I am living; it reminds me of the noble existence I am called to live. It transforms the ordinary struggles of life into epic battles for victory. It turns a quiet evening with Leslie and Hudson into a peaceful meadow of bliss. Who needs Hollywood when the drama of a lifetime is right at your fingertips?

Take some time to adopt your own personal sacred code of honor in relationships with the opposite sex. Write down your commitment, and by the grace of God, treat it with sacred honor—even at the cost of your own pleasure or desires. Prove yourself worthy of your future spouse's trust. Don't just wistfully dream about a fairy tale, about becoming a powerful warrior or a noble princess—it's the life that God has called you to live, starting right now. Honor Sacred's position in your life, and get ready for the most amazing existence you could ever imagine.

God loves Eric Ludy too much to allow him to believe that Mr. Purity and Sacred have concluded their work in his life and that he has already fully explored the outer reaches of Great Sex. And God loves you too much to allow you to fritter your life away with the likes of Jimmy the Shrimp and Imposter Sex at the helm.

So my advice to you is this: ask Jesus to begin His work today inside your life. And if you've already started that process, then ask Jesus to introduce you to Mr. Purity and Sacred in all their fullness. I promise you will love them!

More About
Mr. Marvelous

When you personally encounter Mr. Marvelous, you can't help but be inspired to become a better man—noble, honorable, valiant, heroic, romantic, sensitive, and a more accurate picture of the Ultimate Man—Jesus Christ. But just as Mr. Purity is often misrepresented and misunderstood, most of us don't see Mr. Marvelous for who he really is. All too many modern guys have written off Mr. Marvelous as outdated, extreme, and unrealistic.

After I interviewed Mr. Marvelous, I thought back to a conversation I'd had a few months earlier with my buddy Kip as we sat munching sandwiches at a local deli. Kip was complaining to me about the ruthless attack on men in our modern culture. "Every TV show portrays guys as stupid, unintelligent oafs," he griped, his face turning red with outrage. "And it's not just the media—all the women in my life are constantly making sarcastic comments about how insensitive and selfish men are! Women are bashing men like crazy these days. How is a guy supposed to become a real man when women won't even give him the chance?"

Kip's voice had accelerated in volume as he spoke, and his words attracted the attention of Chad, a shaggy-haired, guitar-wielding young man sitting behind us. He turned his chair around, eager to join in Kip's venting of emotional steam. "Hey, man, I know exactly what you mean!" he declared, reaching out his palm to receive Kip's high-five of the afflicted brotherhood. "My girlfriend has these completely unrealistic expectations of what a guy should be. She gets disappointed and complains if I'm not the knight in shining armor she's always wanted. How's a guy supposed to handle that kind of pressure?" He shook his head mournfully and strummed a few angst-ridden chords on his guitar.

Both Kip and Chad, like many modern guys, are all too eager to blame women as the source of their masculine woes. But let's take a closer look at why women really treat guys the way they do.

Women grow up dreaming of a knight in shining armor—a heroic warrior poet who will cherish and appreciate them. It's a healthy, Christ-built desire that is placed inside every feminine heart. But we live in a world controlled by Jimmy the Shrimp; a world tainted by sin and selfishness. As women encounter manhood in today's world, their Christ-given desires for true men are not fulfilled. Their feminine dreams for a heroic knight begin to fade. And one of two responses toward men usually emerges as a result.

One response is that they become hurt, disappointed, and bitter against men to the point where they won't allow guys to be anything but burping, scratching, insensitive oafs. Their mocking sarcasm, though it is a form of self-protection, makes life miserable for the poor chaps like Kip, who want to rise above the status quo but feel paralyzed and held back by jaded femininity.

A second response women have is to keep holding out for a higher standard, hoping that the men in their life will intrinsically understand the deepest longings of their feminine heart. And they get frustrated, hurt, and disappointed when guys let them down. Often they resort to nagging or manipulation in an attempt to change men—which typically causes a guy to dig in his heels and stubbornly declare, "Hey babe, I am what I am—take it or leave it!"

Certainly modern femininity has not excelled at creating the right atmosphere for Mr. Marvelous to be seen in all his glory. But women are not the source of the problem. They are merely reacting to the lack of Marvelous Manhood all around them. Yes, it is true that most women's attitudes toward men are tainted by the work of Jimmy the Shrimp. But a woman's desire for real men should not be ignored, resented, or mocked. Rather, it should be the fuel that sparks our fire to pursue true manhood at all costs. Not so that we can silence the nagging voices of modern women—but so that we can become the spectacular demonstrations of God's glory that we were destined to be.

During my interview with Mr. Marvelous, he said something I'll never forget. "A man proves he is a true man when he stands up in the face of mocking, disillusioned, nagging, criticizing femininity and showcases a version of Marvelous Manhood that will stop them in their tracks. A true man does not become angry, discouraged, or defensive by the jaded attitudes of women. He does not use women as an excuse for his lack of real masculinity. Rather, he rises up and, through the enabling power of God, becomes the strong, noble, heroic, dignified, gallant warrior-poet he was created to be."

Men have been trying to blame women for their masculine failures since the beginning of creation. Remember Adam in the Garden? When God confronted him about his sin, Adam protested, "The woman whom thou gave to be with me, she gave me of the tree, and I did eat" (Gen. 3:12). But Jesus portrayed a completely different pattern for masculinity. Though His Bride was unworthy and full of faults, though she mocked and rejected Him, though she did not believe or accept His love for her—He did not hold any of that against her. Instead, He humbled Himself and gave up His very life to set her free.

When it comes to our masculinity, it is Jesus, not Adam, we are meant to imitate. Jesus doesn't make excuses. He doesn't put the blame on His Bride. He doesn't evaluate whether she is worthy or whether she has the right attitude toward Him. He lays down His life for her, without condition, without strings. *He* takes the blame. Jesus is the ultimate demonstration of heroism and meekness, of sensitivity and strength. He is the truest Mr. Marvelous there is. No, we won't reach the perfection of Christ's example this side of heaven. But why should that hold us back from coming as close as we possibly can? I don't know about you, but I am striving to be the best husband, the best father, and the most marvelous man in the entire world. Why not aim high? There's not much competition these days. And besides, we have the supernatural enabling power of God's Spirit on our side!

Guys, it doesn't matter whether women's expectations

toward men are unrealistic. It doesn't matter if modern femininity mocks, criticizes, or jokes about men being insensitive oafs. If Jesus had considered the worthiness of His Bride, He never would have sacrificed His life in the most heroic demonstration of love this world has ever seen.

When you rise up and embrace Mr. Marvelous in all his fullness, you will be amazed at how females all around you will change—everything from their attitude to their respect level for men will be affected for the good. But don't let that be your motive and don't put conditions on your behavior. Determine to showcase God's glory through your manhood, so that you can honor the One who gave everything for you. Yes, the standard of Mr. Marvelous is humanly impossible. But don't let that stop you. God's Spirit is ready to equip, empower, and enable you to showcase a version of manhood that will shake this world for eternity.

Note: If you are looking for practical ways to begin applying Marvelous Manhood to your life, take some time to read the incredible display of masculinity in Job 29. Then ask God's Spirit to enable you to begin applying those qualities to your life, starting today. God is very eager to answer a prayer like that! I'd also recommend my book *God's Gift to Women*—but remember, as Mr. Marvelous said, it's only a starting place.[1] Marvelous Manhood truly is an endless frontier!

More About Feminine Grace

The words of my princess make me a prince.

It never ceases to amaze me how Leslie's sweet words, her delicate grace, and her soft feminine touch upon my heart can imbue such incredible strength into my soul. After reading one of her patented love letters, I am ready to slay ferocious dragons and storm medieval castles.

Leslie, to me, is an amazing picture of Feminine Grace, of beauty and strength. She speaks words of tender compassion when they are needed, but she is not afraid to be a strong and courageous messenger of God's truth. She will gently caress my cheek when I am discouraged, but she doesn't hesitate to administer a good swift (but loving) kick in the rear end when I need it!

There is no denying it; Feminine Grace wields a tremendous power. It's a power that can be used either for good or for harm in a man's life. Leslie could destroy me with her words. She could choose to be nagging, critical, and demeaning toward me, and watch my confidence as a man melt away. But instead, she chooses to allow Sacred to shape and mold her feminine power into a beauty and strength that builds mighty muscles of marvelous manhood within my life. And the fact that she acknowledges that she is not a finished work—that she has only begun to explore the endless frontier of Christ-shaped womanhood—makes her femininity all the more appealing.

I sing the praises of my wife everywhere I go. I want the world to know what a blessed man I am, even if my overly sentimental sonnets make people squirm. Often when I speak about the feminine grace that Leslie exudes, women think warily, *Sure, I could be a great woman too if I only had a guy spouting sonnets about me and writing sappy love letters to me all day! Of course Leslie is a great wife, Eric, with a husband like you who is passionately (sickeningly) in love with her!*

Just as Mr. Marvelous is often seen as unreachable, so is Feminine Grace. One of the biggest lies young women believe is that they cannot excel at womanhood unless they are surrounded by fawning men—that they cannot truly become a stunning princess unless they are adored and appreciated by a gallant prince.

Though Leslie encountered Sacred and Feminine Grace in a whole new way through the course of this book, the truth is that she invited these lovely companions into her life long before I came into the picture. During our love story, while other girls were aggressive and flirtatious, Leslie possessed an enchanting mystery that took my breath away. While other girls shamelessly took the role of initiator in pursuing guys, Leslie waited for a man who would rise up and be a Christlike leader. While other girls traded in feminine elegance for trashy seductiveness, Leslie carried the lovely dignity of Sacred and Purity. While other girls grew impatient and took their love life into their own hands, Leslie put all of her confidence in God's perfect timing.

It was Leslie's Feminine Grace that first drew me to her; she was a stunning reflection of Christ in her femininity. And she cultivated all of those qualities before she even knew my name. It was not me who enabled Leslie's Feminine Grace to come alive; it was Christ.

Even now, in our marriage, though I do my best to cultivate and nurture her beauty, Leslie's source of radiance does not come from her husband's love. If I died and she was left alone— her womanly strength and beauty would not fade. Again, it is not my adoration and appreciation of her that causes her to exude with inner loveliness—rather, it is the love of her true Bridegroom, Jesus Christ.

Encountering the mediocre state of masculinity today can cause disappointment and disillusionment in the feminine heart. You dream of a knight in shining armor, but the guys that surround you are a far cry from the fairy tale version of manhood.

You have a choice to make.

You can choose the common road patrolled by Jimmy the Shrimp. You can give in to your disillusionment and become jaded and bitter toward men; you can gripe and complain and try to manipulate the guys in your life to become nobler and more heroic.

Or you can choose the Sacred path, a path very few women ever find. The Knight of all knights, Jesus Christ, awaits your hand in marriage. He alone can adorn you with Feminine Grace that will win the heart of a noble prince and transform masculinity as you know it today.

Remember my buddies Kip and Chad (appendix C)? Their attitude toward women is laden with selfishness, laziness, and self-pity. All too many women fall into the very same trap, pointing the finger of blame toward the opposite sex instead of rising up and becoming the magnificent displays of femininity they were created to be.

But this doesn't need to be your story.

Ladies, it doesn't matter how ugly, unworthy, or unappreciated you feel; it doesn't matter how many men have hurt you, or how deeply; you are not beyond the reaches of Christ's transforming Feminine Grace. To Christ, your life is full of amazing feminine potential. To Him, you are priceless—worth even His very life. And the reality of Christ is the only reality that matters.

Jesus Christ stands ready and eager to take your femininity and transform it into a breathtaking demonstration of His grace, beauty, and strength. All you must do is allow Him to.

Note: If you are looking for practical ways to allow Christ to equip you with Feminine Grace, take a few moments to read the story of Mary of Bethany in Luke 10:38–42, and allow God's Spirit to show you how you can begin applying that amazing version of womanhood to your life, starting today. I would also highly recommend Leslie's book *Authentic Beauty*.[1] Great Womanhood is truly a fathomless frontier!

Notes

Chapter 19: What About . . . ?
1. Eric and Leslie Ludy, *The First 90 Days of Marriage* (Nashville: Thomas Nelson, 2006).
2. Eric and Leslie Ludy, *When God Writes Your Love Story: The Ultimate Approach to Guy-Girl Relationships* (Sisters, OR: Multnomah, 2004), 36.
3. Eric and Leslie Ludy, *A Perfect Wedding: Inviting the Author of Romance to Make Your Day Beautiful* (Eugene, OR: Harvest House Publishers, 2006). Used by permission.
4. Eric Ludy, *God's Gift to Women: Discovering the Lost Greatness of Masculinity* (Sisters, OR: Multnomah, 2003), 182–183.

Appendix A: Taking the Purity Test
1. Amy Carmichael, *God's Missionary* (Fort Washington, PA: Christian Literature Crusade, 1998), 39. Used with permission.

Appendix B: Taking the Sacred Test
1. Eric and Leslie Ludy, *When God Writes Your Life Story: Experience the Ultimate Adventure* (Sisters, OR: Multnomah, 2004).

Appendix C: More about Mr. Marvelous
1. Eric Ludy, *God's Gift to Women: Discovering the Lost Greatness of Masculinity* (Sisters, OR: Multnomah, 2003).

Appendix D: More about Feminine Grace
1. Leslie Ludy, *Authentic Beauty: The Shaping of a Set-Apart Young Woman* (Sisters, OR: Multnomah, 2003).

Teaching True Love to a Sex-at-Thirteen Generation:

Today's young people are in desperate need of parents who understand the intensity of the battle they are in and who are equipped to help them experience something better than the cultural norm. This poignant and practical book equips parents to motivate their kids to pursue something better than the culture's version of love, prepare them now for a romance that will last a lifetime. A relevant and timely message that no parent or leader should miss!

The First 90 Days of Marriage:

Lay the foundation now for a marriage that will not merely survive but thrive for a lifetime. This book is full of practical insight, such as "How to Stay Madly in Love Through Life's Ups and Downs," "How to Tackle Life as a Team," and "How to Build the Ultimate Romantic Sanctuary." Whether you are soon to be married, have been married many years, or simply want to gain God's perspective for marriage in your single years, you'll greatly benefit from this powerful book.

authentic *girl*
MINISTRIES
In every generation there are a few ...

Tools to equip you in your set-apart journey...

AUTHENTIC GIRL NATIONAL CONFERENCES WITH LESLIE LUDY

- take the message of *Authentic Beauty* deeper

AUTHENTIC GIRL FELLOWSHIP GROUPS

- connect with other set-apart young women in your community

AUTHENTIC GIRL MAGAZINE

- cultivate Authentic Beauty in every aspect of your life

VISIT www.authenticgirl.com
TO LEARN MORE!